Cover art by *Jane A. Evans*

Whispers from the Other Shore

A Spiritual Search - East and West
Ravi Ravindra

This publication made possible with the assistance of the Kern Foundation

THE THEOSOPHICAL PUBLISHING HOUSE
Wheaton, Ill. U.S.A.
Madras, India / London, England

For additional information write to:
The Theosophical Publishing House, 306 West Geneva Road,
Wheaton, Illinois 60189.

A publication of the Theosophical Publishing House, a department
of the Theosophical Society in America.

Library of Congress Cataloging in Publication Data

Ravindra, Ravi.
    Whispers from the other shore
    "A Quest original" — T.p. verso
    Bibliography: p.
    Includes index.
    1. Spiritual life.   2. Ravindra, Ravi.   I. Title.
BL624.R38   1984   291.4   84-40164
ISBN 0-8356-0589-2 (pbk.)

Printed in the United States of America

To Mrs. Louise Welch and J. Krishnamurti
with affection and gratitude for them,
and with an appreciation of their differences

Contents

Preface ix
Acknowledgments xv
1 The Spiritual Quest 1
2 Religion as Living Experience 19
3 The Indian Tradition 28
4 The Judaeo-Christian Tradition 43
5 The Parting of the Ways 57
6 From the Alone to the Alone 83
Notes and References 117
Glossary of Indian Words 131
Selected Bibliography 135

I am dead because I lack desire;
I lack desire because I think I possess;
I think I possess because I do not try to give.
In trying to give, you see that you have nothing;
Seeing you have nothing, you try to give of yourself;
Trying to give of yourself, you see that you are nothing;
Seeing you are nothing, you desire to become;
In desiring to become, you begin to live.

René Daumal

Let not worldly prudence whisper too loudly in thy
ear, for this is the hour of the unexpected!

Sri Aurobindo

God cannot know himself without me.

Eckhart

Preface

"The Kingdom is within you and it is outside you,"
said Jesus Christ in the *Gospel According to St.
Thomas*. "When you know yourselves, then you will
be known; and you will know that you are the sons of
the living Father. But if you do not know yourselves,
then you are in poverty, and you are poverty."

Central to the spiritual search is the question Who
am I? Asking this is to open oneself to the mystery of
one's being—with all its confusions and pretensions as
well as its aspirations and possibilities. To be alive to it
now is to be present at the creation of this moment.
When I am not in question to myself, I do not exist,
except as a memory in unconscious time.

Since it is of perennial significance, this question
has been raised perennially, in various idioms and
various forms. At different periods in history, spiritual
search has been expressed in philosophies, psychologies, arts, and above all in religions; by these ways
seekers have been called and helped in sustaining and
deepening their quest. With time wayfarers and pil-
grims are in general replaced by believers and officials
prizing the security of their positions. Rather than the
path leading to openness and vulnerability to truth, we
find too many frozen statements and doctrines claiming to provide the answers.

With the inescapable influences of the family and

society, we acquire some sort of socio-philosophical religion. Whether we are believers or doubters, this religion can become a veil between ourselves and what is, at the same time as it acts as a bulwark against forces of chaos and darkness. If we would penetrate this veil, we must understand its peculiar fabric and coloration; in this, a comparative study of different traditions can be of immense value. It may even be possible to hear, in the interstices of religious forms, whispers and hints from the other shore—clarifying and deepening one's search. Religions are like life itself, full of haunting promises, massive failures, and occasional illuminations; they contain the possibility of searching for truth but generally settle for secure formulations. Ultimately, however, religions are what they are; it is the meaning and sense of our own existence that are at stake. It is for the sake of our own deepest self that we must ask questions about the nature and purpose of our being: Who are we? What do we seek? What help, if any, can we find? Why are we here? What must we serve?

It is useful to view religions at three distinct levels: quantitative, theological, and experiential. At the *quantitative* level, with which most of the scientific studies of religion are concerned, church officials worry about the declining attendance in the pews and in the seminaries; they devise schemes of social relevance and organize interesting groups to attract the youth and the dissatisfied. To be sure, these institutional forms of religion serve many functions, but rarely is it the nurturing of the spiritual search. At this level of temples, officials, numbers, policies, sermons, and services, all religions basically amount to the same: the believers are provided with solace, rituals, and dogmas by which their existence can be made bearable; the harsher aspects of reality are filtered out and the faithful are left with the comfortable illusion that they are especially entrusted with truth here and chosen for great glory in the hereafter.

At the *theological-philosophical* level, with its focus on logical and systematic discourse, there are pronounced divergences between the two traditions to be considered here. The Hindu-Buddhist tradition is almost exclusively inward-oriented with enlightenment as the goal for each person, to be attained by his° own efforts, whereas the Judaeo-Christian tradition is generally other-oriented and based on revelations to especially chosen prophets of God. For the former, the starting point is the individual—suffering, searching and seeking deliverance; the latter starts from God who reveals his commandments to which man responds. However, the verbal, discursive, philosophical point of view, like all other points of view, can be but partial: spiritual becoming is not merely a matter of rational examination of doctrines and propositional truths—however recondite and quintessential.

The direct *experiential* level, which is prior to any theological-philosophical systematization, calls for a discipline of body, mind, and soul, for an integration of all of one's energies. The aspirant becomes a pilgrim on the way to wakefulness and being. Knowledge along this path has a transforming character, for here, as Parmenides said: "Only when transfigured and reborn in the spirit can one know the Old One."

At this level, there are no essential differences between the two streams; both ultimately derive their vitality from the remarkably similar experiences of sages and saints. The significant feature of these

_____
°Masculine pronouns (he, him, his) are used for convenience only and are meant to include women as well.

experiences appears to be the surrendering of one's ego-self to a greater will. This will is at a higher level *above* oneself (Biblical tradition) or at a deeper level *within* oneself (Indian tradition). Linguistically this leads to markedly different theologies, but for an integrated self, which every spiritual tradition insists is higher than discursive reason, our usual distinction and dichotomies of past and future, within and without, subject and object, good and evil, lose their rigidity and importance. When the Spirit has taken over the guidance and authorship of one's actions and words, the individual ego is transcended and the linguistic and ethical opposites are reconciled. Both traditions regard this spiritual reorientation, or rebirth, as necessary for liberation—their first and last purpose.

Neither can one ignore the remarkable similarities at the primary, experiential level or the profound differences at the secondary, philosophic level between these two major traditions. What one chooses to emphasize depends to a large extent on one's point of view and purpose. Having spent half of my life in the Western world and half in the Eastern, I am culturally neither, or both. In any case, I am convinced that no culture has a monopoly on either stupidity or wisdom. Every culture has had, and will continue to have, great teachers and profound insights. One of the characteristics of our times is that now it is more difficult to be parochial than at any other time in the past. It requires a special sort of imperviousness these days in order to ignore the existence of other great cultures and religions, and thereby impoverish oneself rather than becoming heir to the wisdom of all mankind. While approaching the various religious traditions, my interest is not to prove the superiority of one or the other; one could prove anything, depending on the levels from which one gathers data. My interest in the study of these traditions is primarily practical and spiritual. What insight can the traditions provide into my own situation, so that I can live more abundantly and rightly?

In the first chapter I present the nature of the universal spiritual quest and realization as expressed by the sages and prophets in these two traditions. The next four chapters deal with the divergence of the theologies and religions as they have emerged in the process of rationalization and organization of these seers' words and deeds. In the last chapter, I return to the theme of the first, but more from the practical point of view of those who, like the author, are on this side of the veil and are seeking. It is clear that we need help in listening to and pursuing our own questions, and in keeping them from becoming merely academic and verbal. Such help cannot come primarily, and certainly not exclusively, from science, philosophy, religion, or psychology. Although the truth about ourselves is not independent of the truth about the cosmos, unless we find a place of reconciliation and discernment within ourselves, we are bound to be lost in contradictions, words, and facts without meaning. The traditions, in fact, do speak about such reconciliation, but it remains for each one of us to discover which forms have become mere slogans and doctrines for us and which ones still retain the fire of genuine practical knowledge and experience.

In this study, I have attempted to understand what is essential and general. Clearly the details are important; but contrary to the prevalent intellectual opinion, I do not think that one can, except in a limited context and for a limited purpose, proceed from detailed investigations of parts to an understanding of the whole. However unscientific it may appear to some, in my experience the meaning and significance of the details cannot be grasped unless one has some understanding of the central question. If the general theme is of interest, then one can decide which aspects need to be studied, externally or experientially, in detail.

What follows is essentially a personal attempt to meet the two major religious traditions with the basic question, Who am I? My temerity in offering it to fellow seekers comes from the recognition that it is not merely a personal question but is of universal concern. This effort (in the sense of the original meaning of the word *essay*, an *attempt*) had to be made; I needed to do it. In the process, I gathered many insights, and many mysteries were deepened and enlivened for me. Friends persuaded me that some of these can be of value to others and it should be published. But there are no theses here, no arguments or conclusions. To be sure, there are ideas, mostly gathered from sacred literature and arranged according to my understanding. The reader should be warned, as a helpful reviewer remarked, that this book does not lead anywhere; it is a long meditation on and around a theme. The theme is the mystery—of one's own existence, in the spirit in which the psalmist asked, "What is man, that thou art mindful of him?"

Acknowledgments

My own spiritual quest has been nurtured and sustained by many influences both in India and the West, the two geographical and cultural regions where I have spent almost an equal amount of time in my life. I wish, with particular fondness and gratitude, to recall my meetings with three wise people: J. Krishnamurti whom I met one magical afternoon two decades ago in his temporary abode, perched over the sacred Ganga near Varanasi, and many times since then; Lama Anagarika Govinda whom I visited on several days in his beautiful Kesar Devi Ashram in the Himalayas; and Mrs. Louise Welch who gave me so much of her time and attention in New York and elsewhere, in helping me understand the teachings of G. Gurdjieff, and who made it possible for me to work with Madame Jeanne de Salzmann in Paris. They have been like the angels of the Lord with whom I have felt inwardly obliged to wrestle. The fact that I have remained recalcitrant has not diminished their love for me nor my gratitude for them.

Professors Huston Smith of Syracuse University, J. B. Hardie of the Atlantic School of Theology, A. Hilary Armstrong, F. Hilton Page and W. J. Archibald of Dalhousie University, and the late Professor Walter Kaufmann of Princeton University kindly read earlier drafts of this manuscript and made very helpful comments. In particular, Professor Armstrong pointed out several parallels with Plotinus. I owe them all a great deal; but the errors and exaggerations that remain are wholly mine.

My wife served variously as a critical editor, typist and listener—always with love. Other friends have helped with questions, comments, and encouragement.

Research Grants from the Canada Council (1970-72) and Dalhousie University (1972-73) are gratefully acknowledged. A part of this work was written when I was a Visiting Fellow in the Program of History and Philosophy of Science at Princeton University in 1968-69, on fellowships awarded by the Canada Council and the Killam Foundation. It was revised at Columbia University, in 1973-74, where I was a Visiting Scholar in Religion on a Fellowship for Cross-disciplinary Study awarded by the Society for Values in Higher Education; and was published by the Shaila Press in 1976 under the title *From the Village to the Mountain: Spiritual Search—East and West*. What follows is an expanded version of that publication.

Some of the material in the book has been developed and elaborated elsewhere in scholarly journals, for example:

"Self-surrender: the Core of Spiritual Life," *Studies in Religion*, v. 3, no. 4, 1974.

"Time in Christian and Indian Traditions," *Dalhousie Review*, v. 51, no. 1, 1971.

"Is Religion Psychotherapy?—an Indian View," *Religious Studies*, v. 14, 1978.

"The Dimensions of the Self: *Buddhi* in the *Bhagavad Gita* and *Psyche* in Plotinus," *Religious Studies*, v. 15, 1979 (with A. H. Armstrong).

"Perception in Yoga and Physics," *Re-Vision*, Spring 1980.

1

The Spiritual Quest

The struggle to know who I am, in truth and spirit, is the spiritual quest. The movement in myself from the mask to the face, from the personality to the person, from the performing actor to the King of the inner chamber, is the spiritual journey. To live, work, and suffer on this shore in faithfulness to the whispers from the other shore is spiritual life. To keep the flame of spiritual yearning alive is to be radically open to the present, and to refuse to settle for comforting religious dogma, philosophic certainties, and social sanctions.

Who am I? Am I Judas, am I Jesus? Out of fear, out of desire, I betray myself. I am who I am not. I cover my face with many masks, and even become the masks. I am too busy performing who I think I am to know who I really am. I am afraid: I may be nothing other than what I appear to be; there may be no face behind the mask. I decorate and protect my mask, preferring a fanciful something over a real nothing.

1

I cling to the herd for comfort. Together we weave varied garments to cover our nakedness. We guard the secret of our nothingness with anxious agility lest we should be discovered.

Occasionally, I hear a voice uttered in some dark recess of myself. Sometimes it is the soft sobbing of a lonely child. At other times, the anguished cry of a witnessing conscience. At yet other times, it is the thundering command of a king. Who are you? I ask. I AM.

What am I asking when I ask Who am I? What sort of *answer* would be acceptable? Do I want a chart of my genealogical and social relations? A list of my racial and biological characteristics? A catalogue of my psychological features—my likes and dislikes, desires and fears? These are all the things that shape my personality. But whose personality is it? Who wears this mask? In response to a little knock at the door of my consciousness, I ask Who is it? No naming—son of God, Self, *Atman*, Krishna—is sufficient. What I seek is to see the face of the one who calls.

Who am I? does not ask for an enumeration of scientific facts: it expresses a certain restlessness, groping, and exploration. It is the beginning of a movement towards light, towards seeing things clearly, as a whole. It is the refusal to remain in the dark—fragmented and on the surface of myself. It is a state of searching for meaning, comprehensiveness, and depth. It is the desire to wake up.

Soon I betray this impulse and am lulled back to sleep by comforting caresses and fairy tales. I sleep, dreaming of great adventures and questing for the hidden treasures. Many journeys, many peaks, and the lions guarding the mountain passes. For a moment I wake up—to find myself a prisoner of what I know and what I am. Even finding the door of my little prison open, I stay in it, afraid to leave, counting and recounting my possessions and my testimonials.

I share many walls with others. With vigor and imagination, I collaborate with others in building the castles of science, art, philosophy, and religion in which we may rest secure, unmindful of our ignorance of who we are, why are we here, and why we do what we do. The silent witness inside me asks: What do you seek?

AWAKENING

All spiritual traditions thus diagnose the human condition: man is asleep and his life—ambitions, fears, activities—are governed by vast forces, outside of his will or control. He can, with instruction, grace, and effort, wake up, see his situation as it is, and begin to listen to his inner voice.

Gurdjieff tells an Eastern tale about a very rich and mean magician who had a great many sheep. But he did not want to hire any shepherds nor erect fences around the pastures where the sheep grazed. Often the sheep wandered away into the forest and were lost, and some of them ran away, for they knew that the magician wanted their flesh and skins. At last the magician thought of a remedy. He hypnotized his sheep and suggested to them that no harm would come to them because they were immortal, that the magician was a good master who would do anything for his flock, and that even if anything were to happen to them it certainly would not be just then and they need not worry about it. Furthermore, the magician suggested to his sheep that they were not sheep at all: to some he suggested that they were lions, to others that they were eagles, to others that they were men, and to some that they were magicians like himself. Under the influence of hypnotism the sheep believed the magician, who could now rest without care and worry. The sheep never ran away again and quietly awaited the time when the magician would require their flesh and skins. Meanwhile, they grazed happily on the prescribed pasture without needing either shepherds or fences.[1]

Thus we quietly wait; telling each other our conjectures about the wonderful past or the glorious future, our free will or immortality, our loving Father or the great Teacher, the nature of the electron or the rotation of the galaxy—all in a hypnotic sleep, rarely recognizing the real terror of our human situation.

We discover the dream nature of our ordinary existence only when a shock momentarily wakes us up. When we come to, we realize we were sleeping; soon the soporific forces lull us to sleep again. Most of our life is lived in dreaming, day-dreaming or wake-dreaming, and we see the world through a glass darkly: this is the Vedantist's experience of the thralldom of illusion or *maya*. It is only by lifting this veil of maya that one can become awake, *buddha*. If we open our eyes, we see that in our ordinary existence we are estranged from our real self and that we live in a fallen state. We are sinful because we have missed the mark; we experience suffering, *dukkha*, out of ignorance. We are not what we truly are; having forgotten ourselves, we have mistaken our identity.

The nineteenth century Indian saint Ramakrishna told a story about a tigress who attacked a flock of goats. Shot by a hunter just as she sprang on her prey, the tigress gave birth to a cub and died. The cub grew up in the company of the goats. Following their example, he started eating grass and bleating like them, even when he grew to be a big tiger. One day another tiger attacked the flock and was amazed to see a grass-eating tiger in the flock. When the wild tiger caught up to the grass-eating tiger, the latter began to bleat. The wild tiger dragged the other to the water and asked him to look at his face in the water and see that it was identical to his own. He gave a little meat to the bleating tiger, who had difficulty eating it. Gradually, however, the grass-eating tiger got to know the taste of blood, and came to relish the meat. Then the wild tiger said: "Now you see there is no difference between you and me; come along and follow me into the forest."[2]

We can well imagine the jungle-reverberating sound of the two free tigers roaring! We have forgotten our face, our wild roar, and we bleat—as if we were goats. When we remember ourselves, it is like the prodigal son when he came to himself; this our brother was dead and is alive again, was lost and is found. Miserable though the man may be, he can come alive; he can reorient himself and undergo a radical transformation. With effort, knowledge, and guidance, he can become what he is: "Son of the Most High," partaker of divine nature, and a child of God.[3]

When one begins to wake up, one realizes the inner conflict between two poles of oneself: darkness and light, lower self and the higher self (Plotinus), the little *I* (*ahamkar*) and the real *I* (Atman) of the *Upanishads*, world and God (St John), flesh and Spirit (St Paul). And this battle is waged in the psyche of man; man's mind is the battleground of the *Bhagavad*

Gita. As the *Maitri Upanishad* (6.34:11) says, "Mind, in truth, is the cause of bondage and of liberation." Upward and downward tendencies take hold of us periodically; in turn we affirm and deny our deeper selves. In this cosmic play of vast forces, we squirm like hooked fish.

THE EGO

Central to spiritual life, East or West, is surrendering of the ego. Christ said, "If anyone wishes to be a follower of mine, he must leave self behind."[4] *This,* and not ethics, churches, rituals, or doctrines, is essential. The second birth is only after the displacement of the ego from the center of oneself. One of the main purposes of asceticism, esoteric traditions, and spiritual practices is to help a person see the fact that *by oneself,* as one is, one is a mere nothing. Then he may be able to surrender his ego to the higher will and be reborn—in the Spirit. "In my end is my beginning,"[5] for as a Hasidic saying has it, there is no room for God in him who is full of himself.

What then is the ego? At the base of all our activities, there is some anxiety—physical, social, or metaphysical. Our minds are never quiet; constant scheming, calculating, and worrying produces the incoherent sounds of our internal talking machine. The roots of this universal anxiety are the desire to be something, to become somebody, to claim that one is somebody, and the accompanying fear of the failure of this claim. Corresponding to these, there are inner and outer postures and roles that we imagine for ourselves or we acquire from our conditioning. Then we identify ourselves by these roles. The constellation of these postures, pretensions, desires, fears—conflicting and changing—is the ego. Whatever in me hankers for acquisition, possession, and recognition—demanding *my* comfort, claiming *my* success, prestige, wealth and power—is my ego. We use a single word, but in reality, at the level of the ego, there is nothing permanent or constant, only confused and dispersed multiplicity—like a whole army of drunken monkeys in frenzied agitation, running helter-skelter without direction, aim, or will.

All the actions of the ego are anxiety ridden. Siddhartha the Buddha expressed it simply, as one of his four Noble Truths: The cause of sorrow, *dukkha*, is ignorant craving, *trishna*. Our self-will, nourished by our craving, attempts to fashion the world according to our ego-interest. This absurd enterprise is bound to fail and our self-will suffers. Indeed "nothing burneth in hell except self-will."[6]

Self-will and self-interest dominate our lives and turn the world into a huge bazaar where everyone is shouting at the top of his voice to attract attention and to make his little bargain. Indeed this is why "my kingdom is not of this world."[7] Anything of the world, belonging to the web of ego, is opposed to the life of the Spirit. "Anyone who loves the world is a stranger to the Father's love."[8]

This is not to say that we should stop living in the world and commit suicide, or that we should somehow put up with the world until we die. Rather, it is a matter of basic orientation: it is not the *world* but our *worldliness* that opposes the Spirit. Christ prayed for his disciples, "I pray thee not to take them out of the world, but to keep them from the evil one."[9] It is the evil one who tempts us into selfishness. In the life of a spiritual person, supra-worldliness pervades every act; this transforms everything. One is then not driven by craving and is not under the sway of the world: then one operates under different laws, taking direction from inside, and the most ordinary human activity becomes a sacrament, an act of worship. Action is then pure, simple, and in the present—without anxiety, which always concerns the past or future. A Zen monk asked his master: In order to work in the Tao is there a special way?

> The Master replied: Yes, there is one.
> Monk: Which is it?
> Master: When one is hungry, he eats: when one is tired, he sleeps.
> Monk: That is what everybody does; is their way the same as yours?
> Master: It is not the same.
> Monk: Why not?
> Master: When they eat they do not only eat, they weave all sorts of imaginings. When they sleep they give rein to a thousand idle thoughts. That is why their way is not my way.

As we are, without bearings, our ego-interest does not accord with the interest of our deeper self. We do not first seek the inner kingdom and then only the outer one; in the reversal of the true order, we first strive for the dominion of the world. If necessary, we even deny and sacrifice the higher for the lower. But, "What will a man gain by winning the whole world, at the cost of his true self?"[10] It is the false self, the ego, which is obsessed with winning the world. This ego is what we must overcome in order to be "born again . . . . of the Spirit."[11] Conquest of the ego is indeed victory over the abstracted psychic world of our own making that we inhabit and which keeps us burdened and weighed down. He who has overcome the world is from above and is not of this world; such a one living in the world is not driven by worldly desires or ambitions. He does what is demanded of him from above, not for his personal satisfaction or glory.

The distinctive features of egoism are *I-ness*, sundered from the rest of the universe, and *my-ness*. These are the very core and substance of it, and it is by these that a man "binds himself with his self like a bird in a snare."[12] These are the nuclei around which everything of the world revolves. A man of the world says: I do this, I own that; he is self-centered even when he does good works in the service of others. As long as any activity—praying, meditating, alms-giving—is controlled by one's *I*, it is a selfish activity.

> This have I gained today, this whim I'll satisfy;
> this wealth is mine and much more too will be mine
> as time goes on. He was an enemy of mine, I've
> killed him, and many another too I'll kill. I'm master
> here. I take my pleasure as I will; I'm strong and
> happy and successful. I'm rich and of good family.
> Who else can match himself with me? I'll sacrifice
> and I'll give alms: why not? I'll have a marvelous
> time! So speak fools deluded in their ignorance.[13]

Selfless acts are done only by him who is not under the sway of his *I*, who does not do it by himself or for his self-advancement—on earth or in heaven. He responds to an inner demand which may or may not allow for his own convenience. "I do nothing of myself... I seek not mine own glory... I am not myself the source of the words I speak to you: it is the Father who dwells in me doing his own work."[14]

Thus there are two attitudes concerning oneself; in the first the self is the *initiator*, and in the other the self is an *instrument* which does the bidding of a higher will. The struggle between these two tendencies is the conflict between the profane and the sacred, the two natures of man. A great deal of confusion results from

the fact that in either case—whether self is the author
or a tool—language is used and acts are done by and
through aspects of our ego-selves. We tend to consider
only the immediate appearance and identify ourselves
completely with the ego which usurps for itself the
rights of authorship. Thus we live by and for ourselves
alone, estranged from the person behind the mask of
our personality. For us, Self-realization becomes
myself-realization; the demon of *mine* does not
leave us.

What is usually called individualism is totally
opposed in its essence, to the spiritual point of view.[15]
The same is true of the modern, post-Renaissance
humanism, synonymous with individualism, which
regards the meaning and end of a given human life in
terms of the particular person—his fulfillment, his
glory, his salvation. Ultimately, from this point of view,
the person is responsible only to himself, to his isolated, nuclear ego, sundered from the cosmos. Thus
the individualistic modern man is vehemently self-
centered, acknowledging no higher authority and devoted to self-expression and self-fulfillment—precisely the self which Christ said must be denied in
order to follow him. In a truer individualism, one is
responsible for the nourishing and emergence of the
deeper Self within. This Self, however, cannot be controlled and manipulated by us. We may, in our stillness,
allow it room; only then we may hear and obey it.

The Sanskrit word for ego is *ahamkara* which
literally means "I am the doer." This word clearly expresses the egoistic point of view which according to
the *Bhagavad Gita* (3:27.28) can be maintained only
in ignorance: "Every action (*karma*) is really performed by *Prakriti's gunas* (Nature's constituents).
He who is deluded by ego thinks 'I am the doer.' But
he who has the true insight into the operations of the

gunas and their various functions knows that *gunas* act on *gunas*, and remains unattached to his actions." Everything that we see or sense, including our bodies and our psychic functions, are products of the play of forces of nature. The essence of egotism is for man to think that he is the maker of himself and of his destiny. Fooled by ignorance, we think we run the show, like the tribe whose members believe that the sun rises only because of their daily prayers. We are like kittens convinced that the doors open by the force of our mewing. There is a Hasidic saying that the proud are reborn as bees, for in his heart the proud man says: "I am a writer, I am a singer, I am a great one at studying." What is said of such men is true—that they will not turn to God, not even on the threshold of hell. Therefore, they are reborn after they die. They are born again as bees that hum and buzz: "I am, I am, I am.'[16]

According to a simile used in the *Katha Upanishad* (1.3:3-4), the human body is like a chariot whose steeds are the senses; mind or discursive intellect (*manas*) the reins; soul or contemplative intellect (*buddhi*) the charioteer; and the Self (*Atman*) the owner of the chariot. Buddhi is the integrated intelligence which stands between the human mind and the Spirit, between what is below and what is above, between the individual and the cosmic.[17] It is the will that can orient a human being towards the light of the Spirit and give direction to the mind and the senses. On the other hand, if the senses get unruly like the steeds of a chariot, they affect the mind, which in turn leads to dissipation and fragmentation of the buddhi. The buddhi has an amphibious character: it can dive into and stay in the lower world of matter, or it can soar into the higher realms of the Spirit. In the first case, man is led into conflicting desires, illusion, and darkness. That is sin; that is what causes sorrow. In the other case, there is the possibility of movement towards light, towards understanding, integration, and unity.

Mind and the integrated intelligence (buddhi) both belong to the psyche of man and, along with his body, are the determinants of his individuality which with effort and help can serve a higher purpose. Belonging to man's material nature, they represent his particularity—the specific collocation of forces and the peculiar combination that distinguishes him from others. This is the field of individual deeds, memories, and thoughts; this is the realm of space, time, and causation; this is the arena of human efforts and knowledge. This is where a man can purify himself, orient himself upward, and make himself available. He can attend to his nets and lay them judiciously; then he must wait patiently, in readiness for what may come.

When he has let his lips be cleansed with "a glowing coal," he sometimes hears the call, "Whom shall I send? Who will go for me?" He may then, if he has the courage, become an instrument, a prophet, and say like Isaiah, "Here am I; send me."[18]

As we are, we are unable to see or to hear or to understand higher reality, for we live in a state of self-preoccupation. If we recognize our situation, we can begin to be open to what is. We have to prepare ourselves to see and to hear—and to be there when we are called. We can do the divine will when we do not do our own. We have a right ordering within ourselves when we can say like St Paul, "I live, yet no longer I, but Christ liveth in me."[19]

SURRENDERING THE EGO

Every spiritual tradition recognizes and attempts to reconcile a deep-seated duality in human nature.[20]

There is the lower self, the separated ego, enmeshed in the world, arrogating to itself the total identity of the person, in conflict with the Spirit. As long as we remain under its sway, we are "estranged from God"[21] and in sorrow. It is, however, possible for us to repent and come to our right mind,[22] to reorient ourselves radically and to allow ourselves to be led by the Spirit. Only then can an inner reconciliation take place. In a dialogue written by Jacob Boehme, we find a very suggestive metaphor:

> *Disciple*: . . . Oh how may I arrive at the unity of will, and how come into the unity of vision?
>
> *Master*: . . . Mark now what I say; The Right Eye looks in you into eternity. The Left Eye looks backward in you into time. If now you suffer yourself to be always looking into nature, and the things of time, it will be impossible for you ever to arrive at the unity you wish for. Remember this; and be on your guard. Give not your mind leave to enter in, nor to fill itself with, that which is without you; neither look backward upon yourself . . . . Let not your Left Eye deceive you, by making continually one representation after another, and stirring up thereby an earnest longing in the self-propriety; but let your Right Eye command back this Left . . . . And only bringing the Eye of Time into Eye of Eternity . . . and descending through the Light of God into the Light of Nature . . . will you arrive at the Unity of Vision or Uniformity of Will.[23]

But, the power of "nature and the things of time" is clearly great, and our assertive ego, supported by all the worldly forces, proclaims itself. Surrendering of the ego begins to appear as suicidal and disastrous—contrary to our ideas about human development and success. We wish to deal with what is higher than us on our own terms. To us it seems that the sage is beside himself and not in his right mind, for he behaves as if he were dead to the world. But, those who "possess the mind of Christ" feel that "the wisdom of this world is foolishness with God."[24] We have to be out of our worldly minds in order to be raised from the dead and made new in mind and spirit.[25] Only if we can leave our lower self behind, and be "crucified . . . to the world," can we be born in the Spirit.[26] As the *Maitri Upanishad* (6.34:6-7) says, "The mind, it is said, is of two kinds, pure and impure, impure from contact with desire and pure when freed from desire. By freeing mind from sloth and distraction and making it motionless, when one attains to the state of no-mindness, that is the last step."[27]

When one is ended, is emptied out of himself, one does not speak primarily as this or that person, with such and such a history. One does not speak then as a particular individual, for Self-realization is not self-expression. The Self is not yet another acquisition or achievement, however sublime. It cannot be won, coerced or violated. The Spirit is no more yours than mine; we cannot possess it. It is the Spirit that is the owner of the chariot. Leaves cannot lay claim to the wind. The Spirit is not private; it is supra-individual and supra-cultural. One who is born of the Spirit does not proclaim himself, for "this man has now become another and is neither himself nor his own."[28]

All that socially or culturally defines such a person is no longer of much significance. He has become a non-entity from a worldly point of view; his kingdom is elsewhere. The Buddha is "neither priest nor prince nor husbandman nor any one at all. I wander in the world a veritable naught . . . useless to ask my kin."[29] Like Melchizedek, he "has no father, no mother, no lineage; his years have no beginning, his life no end.

He is like the Son of God: he remains a priest for all time."[30]

The kind of knowledge that can lead us to the Spirit has a transforming character; in the process we become different. In order to know what is higher than us, we have to *be* higher. In fact, being and knowing are so intimately connected that the *Mundaka Upanishad* (3.2:9) declares: "He who knows the Brahman (Absolute) becomes the Brahman." For Parmenides and Plotinus "to be and to know are one and the same."[31] Opening oneself to the Spirit, then, is already a movement towards being born of the Spirit.

The liberated man, for whom the magical veil of *maya* is lifted, is no longer within the confines of space and time. He who knows the Spirit, who has become the Spirit, is no longer any particular one for he is identified with the very essence of the universal. The Spirit may, however, manifest itself through a given body and mind—through an individual in space-time —but that does not limit it. The ocean may give rise to waves and be active through them, but it is not limited by them. Our ordinary consciousness is only a small window through which we look at reality; from the point of view of higher consciousness, we restrict our vision unnecessarily. If we widen our doors of perception, we can see more clearly, not as we do now. He who is awakened to the Spirit dwells both in time and in eternity; although he is in time, he is not restricted by it. Eternity is not something opposed to time, nor does it mean an infinite temporal duration, continuing on and on forever. No description exclusively in terms of time can be adequate for comprehending eternity, just as no combination of lines in two dimensions can produce a cube; in that sense, the eternal realm is timeless. What one needs is another dimension of consciousness. As long as we remain confined to our ordinary consciousness, we experience and move only in time, having only vague and occasional hints of eternity.

> Men's curiosity searches past and future
> And clings to that dimension. But to apprehend
> The point of intersection of the timeless
> With time, is an occupation for the saint—
> No occupation either, but something given
> And taken, in a lifetime's death in love,
> Ardour and selflessness and self-surrender.[32]

In order to experience the timeless realm, one does not physically die; it is the reorientation of the ego that is necessary. When one is awakened, the tentacles of space-time fall away, and one is time-freed (*kala-vimukta*). Then one does not live in the past or in the future, but now, in the present, fully awake, radically open. Eternity contains time within it, just as a cube includes a square. A consciousness viewing our temporal world from an eternal and universal point of view cannot be limited by our notions of linear sequence of time and causality or of three-dimensional space. To it, past and future events are as clearly comprehensible as the present ones; clearly visible are the objects far and near. "Yesterday I said something that would seem truly incredible. I said: Jerusalem is as near to my soul as the place where I am now standing. Yes, in all truth; what is even more than a thousand miles farther than Jerusalem is as near to my soul as my own body; and I am as sure of this as I am of being a man."[33]

When a person is not confined by space-time, he becomes a seer and a hearer—one who sees and hears subtle things clearly. Whatever is eternal is always present, without beginning or end in time. "If we take eternity to mean not infinite temporal duration but timelessness, then eternal life belongs to those who live in the present."[34] Kierkegaard speaks of us being *contemporaneous* with the eternal, redemptive (though past) deed of Jesus Christ. The temporal order—past, present, and future—does not describe or delimit the eternal order. When one is liberated from time, one says with Aurobindo:

> I have become what before time I was
> A secret touch has quieted thought and sense:
> All things by the agent mind created pass
> Into a void and mute magnificence.[35]

Sages are all agreed that the Spirit is beyond description, ineffable. Just as It is neither red nor non-red, It is neither one nor many, neither plenitude nor void, neither in time nor out of it, neither within nor without, neither this nor that. It is neither nothing nor everything. All categories of thought and description derive their existence and meaning from It, and not It from them. It is not defined or exhausted by any formula or symbol whatever. "By what should one know that by which all this is known? By what . . . should one know the knower?"[36] Thought, knowledge, and language all function in time and can at best comprehend and describe what is temporal, not what is spiritual and therefore eternal. Negligence of this fact is responsible for innumerable doctrinal disputes in religions and for the problems for religion which the philosophers pose. Like fools, we look at the finger which points to the far star and take hold of it as if it were the star.

In order to say anything at all about the distant star, sages have used various symbolic words, such as That, Brahman, God, YHWH, Allah, Suchness, Void, Absolute, Truth, Love, Nothing—all attempts to name the

nameless. So long as these remain only words, concepts and ideas, they are like dead coals without any
flame. At their core, however, they embody the force
of volcanic eruptions; they stand for the "devouring
fire" which one approaches only with fear and
trembling,[37] in order to make sacrifice of one's ego.
He who experiences the baptism under fire may
emerge melted down and reshaped, not as himself,
but as the very Person, as *Purusha*, as the Son of God.
He may rise from the dead to "mature manhood,
measured by nothing less than the full stature of
Christ."[38]

What are we—we who are drawn by divinity and
held down by our selfish concerns, we who hear the
call from the other shore and betray it? The movement from this shore to the other is the spiritual pil-
grimage. Our life touches both the shores, but out of
ignorance and fear we cling to this shore which we
imagine we know and where we feel secure and in
control. We do not know what will become of us and
what we might do if we let go of our usual worldly
props. Lest we make fools of ourselves, we choose to
stay in the familiar prison of our little egos, trying to
strike bargains with the unknown, using coins of piety,
good works, and learning. However, in spite of our
great need for certainty, there just cannot be any
guarantee of what will be revealed when we open ourselves and become vulnerable.

How do some of the major religions diagnose our
situation? What clusters of idioms and concepts do
they use? How are we conditioned by them as we grow
up? What is required from us to recognize their, and
our, surfaces and make a move to the depths?

2

Religion as Living Experience

The spiritual quest and organized religion are related much like love and marriage: they can flourish together or separately. No doubt there can be feigning in matters of love, but counterfeit love does not last long because of the constant giving of oneself that is required. Marriage is another matter; people often marry for reasons other than love. It is a socially sanctioned arrangement which can linger on as a dead, dull habit. There have been awakened men within religions, but also outside of them. Official creeds and theologies have sometimes helped the spiritual search and sometimes hindered it; in general they seem indifferent to it in practice as if their main concerns were primarily social and worldly.

One imagines that the only serious raison d'être of religious organizations, buildings, ceremonies, and dogmas is to help men in their struggle to lead a holy life, a life centered in the Spirit. However, the strength

of worldly forces being what it is, in the religious
sphere as in any other, means and ends often get confused. Institutions and officials not infrequently find
themselves unable to devote their energies to the
sacred task of transforming "old" men into "new"; old
forms often become merely routine and repetitive.
Worse still, what was made for the service of the sacred
can be misused in the service of the profane—sometimes in the name of God and his prophets, sometimes
out of ignorance, and sometimes out of wilful misappropriation. To those innumerable officials, priests,
and pandits throughout history, who traded in
counterfeit spiritual wares for their own personal
glory, safety, or comfort, Jesus addressed these words:

> The scribes and Pharisees . . . preach, but do not
> practice. They bind heavy burdens, hard to bear,
> and lay them on men's shoulders; but they them-
> selves will not move them with their finger. They
> do all their deeds to be seen by men. . . .
>
> Woe to you, scribes and Pharisees, hypocrites! be-
> cause you shut the kingdom of heaven against men;
> for you neither enter yourselves, nor allow those
> who would enter to go in. Woe to you, scribes and
> Pharisees, hypocrites! for you traverse sea and land
> to make a single proselyte, but when he becomes a
> proselyte, you make him twice as much a child of
> hell as yourselves. . . . Woe to you, scribes and
> Pharisees, hypocrites! for you cleanse the outside of
> the cup and of the plate, but inside they are full of
> extortion and rapacity. You blind Pharisee! first
> cleanse the inside of the cup and of the plate, that
> the outside also may be clean. Woe to you, scribes
> and Pharisees, hypocrites! for you are like white-
> washed tombs, which outwardly appear beautiful,
> but within they are full of dead men's bones and all
> uncleanness. So you also outwardly appear
> righteous to men, but within you are full of

hypocrisy and iniquity. Woe to you, scribes and Pharisees, hypocrites! for you build the tombs of the prophets and adorn the monuments of the righteous, saying, 'If we had lived in the days of our fathers, we would not have taken part with them in shedding the blood of the prophets.'[1]

The spiritual effort is essentially towards awakening and rebirth. "Except a man be born again, he cannot see the kingdom of God."[2] In the necessary struggle of the individual with the soporific forces, organized religions have often aided the latter—sometimes unwittingly and with good intentions. In general, mankind seems to thrive on illusions. Most of us have neither the intention nor the internal resources required to make even the beginnings of an effort to rise from our common hypnotic sleep. What we seem to need, after bread and circuses, are solace, comfort, approval, and the belief that a powerful, benevolent and forgiving eye has our affairs under its loving gaze. Any institution that would fulfill these needs prospers in the world. And religious institutions have become prosperous. Pandits and priests, if they suffer at all, are not necessarily suffering in the battleground of the Spirit. In spiritual matters, one sure sign of a counterfeit teaching is that it promises a great deal for very little effort on the aspirant's part: no genuine spiritual path is easy or comforting or self-advancing.

At their core, religions often carry whispers from the other shore; but these delicate sounds are drowned in the worldly din. Their adherents hang on to the words, bones, garments, footprints, and other fossils, reminiscent of a spiritual struggle and triumph. They tend to seek and find only security, falling into a dead routine of litanies, rosaries, genuflections, benedictions, and prayer-wheels—like painting a Rembrandt by numbers. Organized religions are by their very nature idolatrous—worshipping a person, a myth, an image, a place, or a concept. These are precisely what organized religions are organized around. Any of these worshipped objects may be of assistance and use in one's own search; but one has to be constantly on guard. Symbols can so easily shroud, veil, and replace the very reality they are supposed to indicate. The finger that points to the moon can hide it if held too close to the eye.

Nietzsche's lament about a Christian being like everybody else can be equally well applied to the adherents of all other religions. The whole point of spiritual education is to bring about a change in living, in what one does and how. It is not a matter of assenting to some doctrine, dogma, or formula— whether there is a soul or not, whether it transmigrates after death or not, whether the world was created at a definite time or not. As the Buddha said, "whether these views or their opposites are held, there is still rebirth, there is old age, there is death, and grief, lamentation, suffering, sorrow, and despair . . I have not spoken to these views because they are not conducive to extinction of craving, tranquility, and *nirvana*."[3]

Spiritual life is not ultimately a matter of belief in something, although this may be relevant to it at some stage of development. It is a matter of living—searching, struggling, overcoming. It is an effort to become what one ordinarily is not—free. And this transformation is not in some special places and special activities; even the most ordinary act is done differently. A Hasidic pupil was asked whether he visited his master to hear his words of wisdom. "No," came the answer, "I want to see how he ties his shoe laces."[4]

No formula, however solemnly chanted, can by itself bring about understanding and change. "Not everyone that calls 'Christ' Lord, but he that does the will of the

Father, shall enter the Kingdom of Heaven."[5]

We read in the *Vishnu Purana* that those who give up their duties and simply proclaim the name of the Lord, *Krishna, Krishna,* are verily the enemies of the Lord and sinners, for the Lord has taken birth for protecting righteousness. The great saint and poet Kabir says:

> Ages have passed turning the beads,
> But turning of the heart has not occurred.
> Put aside the beads of the hand,
> And turn the beads of the heart.[6]

It is this reorientation of the heart and the mind that is called for, rather than scriptural learning, execution of liturgical details, or doctrinal disputations. It is movement in the new direction—away from selfishness and acquisitiveness—that imparts authority to the words of an awakened person. This authority is not ecclesiastical; it is moral and spiritual authority—from lived experience, not from hearsay or reading. Jesus "taught them as one having authority, and not as the scribes." He spoke of what he knew, and testified to what he had seen.[7]

> There is nothing but water at the holy bathing
>   places; and I know that they are useless,
>   for I have bathed in them.
> The images are all lifeless, they cannot speak;
>   I know, for I have cried aloud to them.
> The Purana and the Korana are mere words;
>   lifting up the curtain I have seen.
> Kabir gives utterance to the words of experience;
>   and he knows very well that all other things
>   are untrue.[8]

Theologians, philosophers, preachers use words, but not "words of experience"; mostly, they have no authority for they have not "lifted up the curtain."

They do not have the wisdom of the other shore; they merely run up and down this very shore, shouting slogans and trying to convert each other, too often in order to increase a sense of their own importance and security.

When a master's life and teachings are codified and formulated, we get at best only a photographic representation of a living person and the experiences he embodied. No amount of historical information or theological interpretation can add up to that Blast of the Spirit, that bloweth where it listeth, destroying and building.[9] Literal truth, however faithfully recorded, remains flat unless vitalized by suffering and experience. The essential transmission of a teaching is not primarily a matter of preserving what the master actually said on any given occasion; it depends more on an inner understanding and assimilation by a few initiates in successive generations. Spiritual truth, more than any other truth, has this intensely experiential quality; unless it expresses itself in a person, even the greatest enunciation tends to degenerate into empty words and slogans. We can enlarge these words into more words by introducing finer and finer verbal distinctions; in the process we build an inner barrier between ourselves and our perceptions. The less touched one is by any genuine experience, the more one clings to words and rituals, and the more possessive and exclusive one becomes. But, spiritual reality is comprehended only by those who do not want to possess it, who are willing to be naked and become vulnerable.

We can, however, start only from where we are. It is a part of the play of forces that we find ourselves where we are—under a given set of conditions and circumstances. The various cultural environments we live in give their own interpretation and coloration to the primordial search. These forms—philosophies, dogmas, rituals—are what men try to possess, over which men quarrel and kill. All religions, like all philosophies, are ultimately lies; the very act of formalizing betrays the spontaneity of the experience. Is it for nothing that both the words *tradition* and *betrayal* are derived from the same root? At best, the traditions present doctrinal and ritualist interpretations of experienced reality. By themselves, without the presence of men aflame with the fire of the Spirit, they cannot perform the task of *re-integration* or *uniting* with higher reality—the root meanings of the words *yoga* as well as *religion*. However, in an individual's effort to realign himself with what is higher, it is indispensable for him to work through himself, for he himself is the very stone out of which will be fashioned the sculpture of new being. In the process, he has to understand and overcome his cultural and religious conditioning.

Religions help to shape and mold our most basic attitudes and aspirations, even for those who do not formally adhere to any religion, or would be loath to acknowledge any such influence. Religion is the most important force in the formation of our cultural filters through which we perceive reality. According to the psychologist Carl Jung, "the religious point of view always expresses and formulates the essential psychological attitude and its specific prejudices, even in the case of people who have forgotten, or who have never heard of, their own religion"[10] He who would know himself must know the peculiar covering of his societal religion, which protects him both from the darkness of moral chaos and from the glaring light of higher truth. When he is prepared, not only to understand truth but also to withstand it, he can set aside the protective covering and *see*. The great saint of the

nineteenth century, Ramakrishna, was frustrated repeatedly by the image of his beloved mother goddess
Kali, to whom he was extremely devoted, in his
attempts to go beyond even her image and form in
order to contemplate the Spirit directly. "Then with
great determination I began to meditate as directed,
and when this time also the blessed form of the Mother
appeared before me, I used my discrimination as a
sword and severed her form in two."[11]

In reality, of course, there are as many religions as
there are individuals—each one according to the
background, need, understanding, and prejudice of
the person. If we remember that at present there are
nearly a billion Christians in the world, and that there
have been many more in the past two thousand years,
we cannot but be struck by the immense variety within
a religious tradition. The most erudite theologian, St
Thomas Aquinas, and a humble peasant or a village
idiot; St Francis of Assisi with overflowing love, and
the Inquisitors; Jesus Christ who sacrificed himself
for the sake of the world, and Adolf Hitler—all these
subscribed to Christianity in their own way. As William
Blake said,

> The vision of Christ that thou dost see
> Is my vision's greatest enemy.
> Thine has a great hook nose like thine,
> Mine has a snub nose like to mine.[12]

Of course, there is an equally immense variety in
other religions as well; we tend to imagine them as
monolithic precisely because we are unaware of their
internal diversity. Still, however different our individual religions are, and however great the diversity
is within each religious tradition, some grouping
together is possible. Our spiritual sensibilities are

conditioned by the common society in which we grow up, the common language we use, and the traditions to which we are exposed.

The two groups considered in the following pages are Judaism and Christianity on the one hand, and the two major Indian religions—Hinduism and Buddhism—on the other. It is obvious that there are profound and irreconcilable differences between the two religions in each of the groups. However, these differences fade when we compare the two major groups with each other. Within the same group, there is a common heritage of sages and prophets and a shared soil of language and culture. There is much smaller difference between the Christian *God* and the Jewish *Yehweh* than between either of these and the Hindu *Brahman*. And, in spite of many internal divergences, there are several ideas—for example, those of *faith* and *uniqueness of history* in the Judaeo-Christian tradition, and of *karma* and *reincarnation* in the Hindu-Buddhist heritage—which are shared within the major groups. In the next three chapters we shall look at the clusters of ideas and concepts in the mainstreams of the two traditions—one underpinning the Western world-view and sensibilities, the other upholding the Eastern—mindful of the fact that now we are trying to subordinate the variety within each tradition and to highlight the differences between two major groups.

3

The Indian Tradition

The central fact in the Indian tradition is that of *samadhi*, "the shining sun to which all Hindu religion points."[1] It is called by various names: *moksha, nirvana, turiya.* Contrasted with the three ordinary states of consciousness—waking, dreaming, and dreamless sleep—is the indefinable state, turiya (the Fourth), about which the *Upanishads* says:

> *Turiya,* say the wise, is not subjective experience, nor objective experience, nor experience intermediate between these two, nor is it a negative condition which is neither consciousness nor unconsciousness. It is not the knowledge of the senses, nor is it relative knowledge, nor yet inferential knowledge. Beyond the senses, beyond the under-

standing, beyond all expression, is the Fourth. It is
a pure unitary consciousness, wherein awareness of
the world and of multiplicity is completely
obliterated. It is ineffable peace. It is the supreme
good. It is One without a second. It is the *Atman*
(Self). Know it alone.[2]

Much of Indian philosophy is a commentary on this
passage. All Indian religions exhort men to strive for
the "supreme good," knowing the Self. Notice that the
supreme good for men in India has no reference to a
God who is over and beyond man. *Turiya*, the highest
state, may be undefinable but it is not beyond possible
experience; it is transcendent only in the sense that it
cannot be subsumed under any categories created by
thought. But it is very much a part of man; ultimately,
there is nothing superhuman about it. This state is
unusual and extraordinary, like a monumental work of
art, but it is not beyond man.

The Upanishadic seer delved very deeply into himself and experienced his Atman—imperishable, un-
changeable, eternal. Externally, the nature gods of
India had given rise to a monotheistic Deity, Brahman
(the Great), who stood above and beyond the Creator,
the Sustainer, and the Destroyer. But now the seers
had uncovered two Absolutes—Atman within, and the
universal essence, Brahman outside. Somewhere at
the banks of the sacred Ganga was then uttered the
exultant affirmation which has reverberated in the
Himalayas ever since: the Atman that is within is
identical with Brahman: Thou art That.[3] The deepest
essence of oneself is one with the essence of all other
beings and of all there is. Ultimately, at the deepest
level there are no *others*. Otherness, separation of oneself from the rest of the cosmos, is a mark of shallow-
ness. Only a superficial person, not the wise, thinks

that he can live by himself and for himself, as distinct
from the Whole.

THE GODS OF NATURE

In India, the long struggle between the spirit of man
and the forces outside him resulted in a realization of
their identity at the most fundamental level. In times
long past, in India, as elsewhere, different powers of
nature were deified, feared, and praised. The *Rig
Veda*, which is the most ancient scripture of India
(dating from 6000 B.C. to 1000 B.C.?)[4] abounds in hymns
invoking or propitiating the rain-god, the wind-god,
the fire-god, the sun-god, and others. The prayers in
these hymns are praises of the greatness and power,
the mysterious nature, and the exploits of these
deities, as well as prayers for various favors. Often the
favors sought are of the nature of material blessings,
such as long life, vigorous offspring, cattle and horses,
or gold. Thus a hymn addressed to one of the gods
says: "Bring thou to us rain from heaven, thou to us
booty undisputed (or strength irresistible), give thou
us thousand-fold food."[5]

Many of the hymns were also chanted in connection
with the performance of rituals and sacrificial rites.
In the very remote past men began to emerge with
strength and power—even over the gods, who were
undeniably identified with the forces of nature. The
power man had over the gods was the power of sacrifice—a notion which developed a thoroughgoing
sacrificial mysticism in the very early stages of the
development of the Vedic culture.[6] If the appropriate
sacrifice was performed according to the very strictly
and elaborately outlined procedure, even the gods
would have to yield. However, the sacrifices had to
be performed with an unflinchingly accurate intona-

tion of the hymns prescribed in the *Vedas*.[7] According to a legend, Tvashtar, the archetypal artisan, had performed a sacrifice for the birth of a son who might kill Indra, the chief of the Vedic gods. But owing to a slight error in pronunciation, the meaning of the prayer was changed and the sacrifice produced a son who was not a killer of Indra but of whom Indra was the killer.

NATURAL LAW

The belief that even the gods are subject to natural laws is fundamental in Indian thinking and is responsible for the development of systematic steps of Yoga for realizing the unity of Atman and Brahman. It is precisely the same spirit which manifests again in the rigorous belief of Gautama Buddha in the chain of cosmic cause and effect. Also, this is the reason why the notion of grace, in the Christian sense, is generally absent in Indian religions. Nothing can escape the law. There are indeed events which are mysterious and appear to us to be miraculous and supernatural. But these are not contrary to law; they are under different laws of which we may not be aware.[8] Thus petitioning to God for something which calls for a suspension of the law is pointless. The only thing to do is to raise one's consciousness so that one becomes aware of the higher-order laws and can act accordingly.

The Vedic commands regarding the precise observance of ritual in the sacrifices and the particular benefits to be derived from these were impersonal commands uniting the concepts of the unalterable law and perfect omniscience; they imply, therefore, the possibility of reaping all the comforts of this life and of the afterlife by submission to these commands and compliance with them. But they involve no lawgiver, no divine person, no author of the universe or of the destinies of human beings, who must be pacified, obeyed, or loved, and by whose grace we receive the blessings of life. We can control our own destinies and have whatever we want, if we only follow the commands. They represent an objective and unalterable law realistically conceived. Vedic literature was considered as having existed by itself from beginningless time, not created or composed by any person, human or divine. The assumption of this mysterious omnipotence of sacrifices, performed by following the authoritative injunctions of the *Vedas*—independently of reason or logical and discursive thought—forms the chief trait of the mysticism of the Vedic type.[9]

The Vedic commandments were regarded as above and beyond reason. Later attempts to intellectualize sacrifices proceeded in the direction of replacement of the actual sacrifices by meditation and reflection. This substitution was believed to produce results which were equally beneficial. Gradually, the concept of sacrifice—with all its attendant benefits—was replaced by the concepts of austerity and effort. Effort according to law was rewarded regardless of the willingness of gods, or even of the good or evil nature of the performer. Indian mythology abounds with stories in which a titan won some special power from one of the gods by his own efforts—usually requiring superhuman strength and perseverance—and later threatens the destruction of mankind.

The titan Hrinayakashipa won the boon that he would not be killed by a god or by a man or by an animal. The demon became immortal and started torturing mankind.[10] (The story has an interesting parallel in the contemporary setting in which an evil genius gets hold of the secrets of nuclear energy!) The gods and men were equally helpless and frightened in the presence of the terrible powers unleashed for destruction.

According to the legend, the gods appealed to Vishnu, the Life Force, responsible for the maintenance of the cosmic order, for intervention. Vishnu moved from his eternal repose and a great cry arose in all directions; then came the terrible silence in which every living creature held its breath, waiting. Even the all-powerful Vishnu could not break the law —the secret of immortality had been wrested by Hrinayakashipa with diligence and knowledge.

The earth trembled and there emerged an awesome form of life—unprecedented, unforeseen, unimagined by men, gods, and demons. Vishnu had incarnated himself as Narasinha—half man and half lion—a creature against whom the demon had not guarded himself. In the boon he asked he had protected himself not only against death at the hands of a known form of life but also against other pairs of opposites, such as above and below, day and night, outside and inside. Vishnu went beyond the opposites and emerged from a pillar connecting above and below, at dusk, connecting day and night, and killed the demon on the threshold—neither (or both) outside and inside. The law cannot be ignored, but a higher law can contain and override it.

MEDITATION AS SACRIFICE

There was a further shift of emphasis on the kind of effort required by man to gain control over the natural forces conceived as gods, whether for immediate material prosperity or for immortality. This shift was inward. Gradually, meditation and reflection replaced sacrificial rites and singing of praise. For example, the oldest *Upanishad* opens with an account of the horse sacrifice and interprets this as a meditative act in which the individual offers the whole universe in sacrifice in place of the horse; by renunciation of the world, he attains spiritual autonomy in place of earthly sovereignty.[11] Parallel with this interiorization of effort was a reappraisal of the numerous deities, resulting in the conception of one Supreme Being. Thus, in the *Rig Veda* (XII, 4.5) we find a verse in which it is said that the deity is one, though he is called by various names. In another *Veda*, the same God is said to become different gods who are but his various manifestations:

> This *Agni* becomes *Varuna* in the evening; in the morning rising he becomes *Mitra*; he, having become *Savita*, goes through the atmosphere; he having become *Indra*, burns through the midst of the sky.[12]

Again, in the *Rig Veda* (X, 121.1 and 2) we find:

> Hiranyagarbha, the golden embryo, arose in the beginning; born, he was one lord of the existent. He supports the earth and this heaven. To what god shall we offer worship with oblation? He who gives breath, gives strength, whose command the gods wait upon, whose shadow is immortality, whose shadow is death. To what god shall we offer worship with oblation?[13]

THE ONE ABSOLUTE

Thus, the Vedic religion shifted gradually from polytheism to what has been called henotheism—which means that when one of the gods was worshipped he was called the Supreme God. And then the Vedic religion developed slowly to monotheism. In the *Atharva Veda* (X, 7) we find a hymn dedicated to the god Skambha where the different parts of this deity are identified not only with the different parts of the material world but also with a number of moral qualities such as faith, austere fervor, truthfulness. All the thirty-three gods of the *Vedas* are contained within him and bow down to him. He is also called Brahman. This crystallization of the concept of the Absolute—the Being of all beings, the Essence of all essences—was the outcome of a great deal of effort in comprehending and systematizing the natural forces and the cosmic processes. We frequently read questions and answers of the following type:

> Who knows truly? Who shall here declare, whence it has been produced, whence is this creation? By the creation of this universe the gods came afterwards; who then knows whence it has arisen?
>
> Whence this creation has arisen; whether he founded it or did not: he who in the highest heaven is its surveyor, he only knows, or else he knows not.[14]

Now what is to be done with this Absolute, Brahman? How is man to relate to The Power? How is man to know it? Without this enquiry, Brahman would have remained only an intellectually derived metaphysical principle underlying a study of the external forces. What is the starting point in spiritual life? The Upanishadic answer to this question is man's self. Therefore, the basic spiritual question is Who am I? This is where one must start in order to know Brahman. The *Upanishads* exhort man to know his true Self, Atman. That is the only way to know Brahman, for ultimately Atman is Brahman:

He who knows that the individual soul, enjoyer of
the fruits of action, is the *Atman*—ever present
within, lord of time, past and future—casts out all
fear. For this *Atman* is immortal. . . . What is within
us is also without. What is without is also within. He
who sees difference between what is within and
what is without goes evermore from death to
death.[15]

MAN'S SOUL AND THE SUPREME SPIRIT

Here is the fundamental turning point in the Indian
tradition: Brahman, the One-without-a-second, is
accessible, knowable through one's self. By uncovering the successive layers within oneself, one can come
face to face with the kernel, the Atman. In the realization of the Atman lies liberation, moksha, and enlightenment, nirvana; this is the goal of man's life.

To know the Atman is supreme and unqualified
good, the highest religion. This knowledge is not
merely rational; to know the Atman is to have one's
whole being transformed for "he who knows the
Brahman becomes *Brahman*."[16] "The *Atman* is not
known through study of the scriptures, nor through
subtlety of the intellect, nor through much learning;
but by him who longs for him is he known. To many it
is not given to hear of the *Atman*. Many though they
hear of it, do not understand it. Wonderful is he who
speaks of it. Intelligent is he who learns of it. Blessed
is he who, taught by a good teacher, is able to understand it. The truth of the Atman cannot be fully understood when taught by an ignorant man, for opinions
regarding it, not founded in knowledge, vary one from
another. Subtler than the subtlest is this *Atman*, and
beyond all logic. Taught by a teacher who knows the
Atman and *Brahman* as one, a man leaves vain theory

behind and attains the truth. Like the sharp edge of a razor, the sages say, is the path. Narrow it is, and difficult to tread."[17]

The important thing is that, however difficult it may be, there is a path—not *the* path because men are different and the creative explorations of their own selves cannot be codified. Precisely because the goal, the truth, or Brahman, is beyond any form whatsoever, all forms of searching are to be respected. What is right and proper for me may not be at all suitable for you because you and I differ greatly from each other. The starting point is my own self; the path is of my own choosing in keeping with my own individuality; the goal is the complete understanding of my innermost essence, the Atman. Religion is not a matter of assenting to some dogma or belief but of striving to unveil the deepest layers of man's being and making enduring contact with them.

Scholars have disagreed for millennia regarding the proper interpretation of the utterances of the Vedic sages. All the orthodox schools and perspectives of Indian philosophy accept the authority of the *Vedas*.[18] But they hold different views regarding the nature of the Atman and the method of its realization.

In some schools, the individual soul is related with the Supreme Spirit as children to a benevolent father who needs to be approached with devotion and self-surrender, much as in Christianity. In some other schools, there is no theistic conception of Deity as the Creator and Sustainer of the cosmos; the spiritual essence of a person is said to be quite separate from the material nature, and the two are eternally self-existent. The Yoga philosophy, formulated by the great sage Patanjali (ca. 200-100 B.C.) accepts the presence of Ishwara, God, and declares that worship of Ishwara and meditation upon him are one of the means of attaining supreme knowledge and liberation. Patanjali does admit, however, that it is not absolutely necessary to believe in Ishwara in order to experience the truth of religion, holding that truth will make itself felt in spite of belief or disbelief provided one follows the practice of yoga. However, according to Patanjali it is easier to gain the end of spiritual enlightenment through faith in Ishwara and through worshipping him and meditating upon him.

The most influential school of thought in India has been that of Vedanta. The word *Vedanta* means, literally, the end of the *Vedas*, with specific reference to the *Upanishads*, the last portion or the essential part of each of the four *Vedas*. The *Upanishads* make no attempt to order their contents but merely record the extraordinary experiences of the seers. In an attempt to systematize and interpret the *Upanishads*, Badarayana (500 B.C. to 200 B.C.?) wrote the *Vedanta Sutras*.[19] From him we learn of other scholars who preceded him in the same attempt but whose writings have not been preserved. These sutras themselves are quite unintelligible without commentaries. However, the *Vedanta Sutras* are unquestionably of great authority, and every important philosopher has written commentaries on them. The best known of these philosophers are Shankara, the exponent of an extreme non-dualism, *advaita*, and Ramanuja, who held to a qualified non-dualism. However, all of the Vedantic schools are agreed that the ultimate goal is certainly the knowledge of Atman-Brahman. The differences arise concerning the methods for the realization of Atman and the interpretation to be given to the ultimate state of liberation—whether Atman becomes the same as Brahman or whether it remains different in essence; whether devotion to Ishwara, the personal God, can lead to final enlightenment or not, and other such questions.[20]

THE BUDDHA

In the vast spiritual and philosophical landscape of ancient India stands the towering figure of Gautama Buddha, the silent sage from the clan of Shakya, radiating wisdom and compassion. According to legend, he was born in the 6th century B.C. in the north of India, near Nepal. Having been forewarned that his son would be either the universal emperor or a Buddha, the father of the future Buddha took measures to keep him enthralled in the pleasures of the world and unaware of the true human situation. But in vain: the Buddha-to-be wearied of these evanescent pleasures when he realized that all beings were plagued by inevitable decay, old age, and death. He renounced his possessions and relations in order to seek the way for the cessation of universal suffering. After studying and practicing austerities under the guidance of some Brahmin ascetics, he abandoned mortification in favor of the Middle Way. He established himself under the Bodhi tree, determined not to rise until enlightened. There he sat, mindful and one-pointed, in the center of the cosmic spiritual struggle, meditating without interruption until he became awakened, and understood the nature of himself and of all other things, and the causes of their appearing and disappearing. The Buddha exulted in a song of victory:

> Seeking the building of the house
> I have run my course in the vortex
> Of countless births, never escaping the hobble
>   (of death)

All is repeated birth after birth!
Householder, thou art seen!
Never again shall thou build me a house
All of thy rigging is broken,
The peak of the roof is shattered:
Its aggregations passed away,
Mind has reached the destruction of cravings.[21]

For the sake of other suffering beings, he then set in motion the wheel of *Dharma*, the teaching leading to enlightenment; at Sarnath (near Varanasi) he gave his first sermon in which he spoke the Four Noble Truths and taught the eight-fold path leading to nirvana and the extinction of sorrow, *dukkha*. Although there are many points of divergent emphasis between the Hindu and the Buddhist traditions, particularly in their later developments, their differences on essential doctrines have sometimes been exaggerated. For the Buddha, just as in the *Upanishads*, "Self is the lord of the self."[22] He advised his disciples to "take refuge in the Self" as he himself had done.[23] In Buddhism, as in Hinduism, ignorance is the root of all evil and suffering. In Hinduism the ignorance is of who we are; in Buddhism of who we are not. In either case, it is only by right knowledge that man can be delivered of this evil and attain nirvana.[24]

LIBERATION FROM WITHIN

In spite of the greatly divergent metaphysical views held by the various scholars and sages, the entire Indian tradition is agreed on one thing: liberation is within oneself and consists in the attainment of the true status of the individual. Belief and conduct, rites and ceremonies, authorities and dogma, are assigned a place subordinate to the art of conscious *self-discovery*. To know the Atman is the only goal. This Atman is beyond words and beyond rituals. "Considering religion to be observance of rituals and performance of acts of charity, the deluded remain ignorant of the highest good," says *Mundaka Upanishad* (1.2.:10). Even scripture ceases to be authoritative when the awakening takes place. These rituals, scriptures, and images can all be helpful in a person's spiritual development, but after a certain stage they may become impediments. Whenever the symbols tend to obscure and supersede the real, the symbols, however precious and dear, must be discarded. Ramakrishna tells us:

> After the initiation, the naked one [Tota Puri, his teacher] asked me to withdraw my mind from all objects and to become absorbed in contemplation of the *Atman*. But as soon as I withdrew my mind from the eternal world, the familiar form of the blissful Mother [Goddess Kali, of whom he was a devotee] radiant and of the essence of pure consciousness, appeared before me as a living reality and I said to the naked one, "It is hopeless. I cannot raise my mind to the unconditioned state and reach the *Atman*." He grew excited and sharply said, "What! You say you can't do it! No, you must!" So saying he looked about him, and finding a piece of broken glass picked it up. Pressing its point between my eyebrows, he said, "Concentrate the mind on this point." Then with great determination I began to meditate as directed, and when this time also the blessed form of the Mother appeared before me, I used my discrimination as a sword and severed her form in two. Then my mind soared immediately beyond all duality and entered into *nirvikalpa*, the non-dual, unitary consciousness.[25]

Ultimately, the Indian's concern is not with any specific dogma, church, or belief. His problem is that of consciousness and transcendental experience. The seers have experienced an order of reality which is more basic and transforming. They exhort everyone to discover this reality in himself.

One of the modern sages of India, Vivekananda, says:

> Do not depend on doctrines, do not depend on dogmas or sects, or churches, or temples: they count for little compared with the essence of existence in man, which is divine; and the more this divinity is developed in a man, the more powerful is he for good. Show by your lives that religion does not mean words, or names, or sects, but that it means spiritual realization.[26]

It is an exacting command; "not a doctrine for the sluggard but for the man who puts forth virile effort."[27] It does not offer peace and security; it insists on personal responsibility and freedom—from the world as well as from God. "Be a refuge to yourselves. Betake yourselves to no external refuge,"[28] said the Buddha.

4

The Judaeo-Christian Tradition

> I will lift up mine eyes unto the hills,
>   from whence cometh my help.
> My help cometh from the Lord,
>   which made heaven and earth.
> He will not suffer thy foot to be moved:
> He that keepeth thee will not slumber.
> Behold, he that keepeth Israel
>   shall neither slumber nor sleep.
> The Lord is thy keeper: the Lord is thy
>   shade upon thy right hand.
> The sun shall not smite thee by day,
>   nor the moon by night.
> The Lord shall preserve thee from all evil:
>   He shall preserve thy soul.
> The Lord shall preserve thy going out and
>   thy coming in from this time forth,
>   and even for evermore.[1]

This psalm beautifully sings the Judaeo-Christian faith and hope in one single God who is all-powerful,

eternally awake, and full of mercy. "Hear O Israel,"
says the Jewish Shema, "the Lord our God, the Lord is
one." He is Omnipresent, Omnipotent, and Om-
niscient; to Him belongs all power and glory. He is
compassionate and just. "Whoever does something
wrong and repents of it he is forgiven at once."[2] The
idea of God's forgiveness is also expressed in the view
that God has two thrones: one for justice and another
for compassion. There is surely justice and the wrong-
doers will be punished, but God will show mercy to
the contrite heart.

All the Palestinian religions—Judaism, Christianity,
and Islam—accept the view that the first fundamental
revelation of God to man was His revelation of the
truth of monotheism to Abraham. "I am the Almighty
God, walk before me, and be thou perfect. And I will
make my covenant between me and thee, and will
multiply thee exceedingly . . . I am thy shield, and thy
exceeding great reward."[3] Already in his dealings with
Abraham, God reveals Himself as One who brings His
people forth, and leads them and guides them. The
prophets from Moses to Jeremiah recognized him
afterwards in this way. Here "we have nothing to do
with the 'projection' of later prophetic experience, but
rather with its simple early beginning. The bringing
forth belongs to the nature of this God as well as [His]
leading."[4]

God sealed the covenant which He made with man
with the giving of a new name, Abraham, to Abram.
The giving of a new name in the Bible always signifies
a momentous event and marks a radical change in
being of the person receiving the new name. In this
case, it was a mark of having been *chosen* by God. The
God who goes forth with these men goes with His
chosen people, who also chose Him. He separates
these people from others who are not chosen, and sets

them in His presence, as He is going with them. In the innumerable vicissitudes in the history of Israel, "this combination, this 'correlation' of guidance and devotion, revelation and decision, God's love for man and man's love for God, this unconditional relation between Him and men remains."[5]

OUR RELATIONSHIP WITH GOD

The relationship between man and God is that between person and Person—it is entirely personal. That is not to say that this relationship is subjective, in the sense of being arbitrary, wishful, egoistic, or idiosyncratic. It is an objective relationship between the very essence of a person, his soul, and God, the highest Person. This God is far from an impersonal principle; He is the Living God who enters into dialogue with His chosen people, who shields them and leads them personally, through His prophets who speak on His authority because He has revealed Himself to them and commanded them to do so.[6] As the prophet Jeremiah said, "Then the Lord put forth His hand, and touched my mouth. And the Lord said unto me, Behold, I have put my words in thy mouth."[7] All the Palestinian prophets—from Abraham through Moses and Jesus to Mohammed—speak on His authority and do His bidding, often unwillingly. The Terrible One seizes them and commands them to go forth in His name, and they obey. Their strength lies in the submission of their wills to the Will of God who rules over human history and intervenes in it when necessary. Yehweh said to Moses, "Behold, the cry of the children of Israel is come unto me: and I have also seen the oppression wherewith the Egyptians oppress them. Come now, therefore, and I will send thee unto Pharaoh, that thou mayest bring forth my

people the children of Israel out of Egypt.... Certainly
I will be with thee.... And I will stretch out my hand,
and smite Egypt with all my wonders which I will do
in the midst thereof."[8]

GOD'S COMMUNITY

The angel of the Lord said to Jacob, "Thy name shall
be called no more Jacob, but Israel; for as a prince hast
thou power with God and with men, and hast pre-
vailed."[9] Innumerable times after this, Yehweh,
described in *Exodus* (3:14) as "I AM that I AM is called
the *Lord, God of Israel*.[10] The name *Israel* no longer refers to one Patriarch but to "His People." God of Israel
is the God of a community—the chosen people. Even
Jesus acknowledges this: "I am not sent," said Jesus,
"but unto the lost sheep of the house of Israel."[11] It is
not known whether *Israel* originally was the name of a
people or a name of a holy confederacy to which the
tribes were gathered together by the leadership of
Moses. In either case they were given the name Israel,
the meaning of which is either "striven with God," as
Jacob did, or "God rules."

Whatever the historical origin of the name of the
community may be, it is clear from the scriptures that
the revelations of God were not a private matter between God and one man—including His revelation as
Jesus Christ, as recorded in the New Testament. God
did not reveal himself for the salvation of one individual soul, however exalted, but to make His will
known to the entire community. The dialogue is always
between God and Israel, even though of necessity it is
addressed to a specially anointed son of Israel. The
same is true in Christianity with regard to the Church
as the mystical body of Christ in which all members
are joined together. A saying has been preserved in

the Russian branch of Eastern Orthodoxy: "A man can be damned alone, but he can only be saved with others."[12]

The relationship between man and God underwent a very significant change from the Old to the New Testament. This change, brought about by the influence of Greek thought, is towards an individualizing of man's relation to God. This individualizing has its roots in the Psalms and Wisdom Literature, and above all in Jeremiah; but its full implications were never realized until the time of St Paul.[13] Many scholars regard this change to be of such fundamental importance that in their view it leads to a radically different type of faith.[14] Significant as these differences are, the fact remains that in the Judaeo-Christian tradition in general there is a great deal of emphasis on the community—whether an individual finds himself born into the community, as in the Old Testament, or chooses to belong to one after his conversion, so that the whole community is exclusively made up of the converted, as with early Christianity. This community of adherents of a common faith is sustained by the religious injunction to love one's fellow believers.

FAITH

As was said, the One who chooses His people is also chosen by them. How do men choose Him? What do they do in return for God's covenant with His chosen people in which He promises to protect them and to lead them? The unequivocal answer, given by the entire Judaeo-Christian tradition, can be summed up in a single word: *faith*. Faith is the wholehearted adherence to the message of the revelations of God, whether it is the Torah, the prophetic utterances, or Jesus Christ himself. Faith is the giving of oneself to be controlled and remade by what commands trust and devotion. Faith consists in the total surrender of oneself in the care of God who "neither slumbers nor sleeps." Faith is radical openness to the plenitude of being, characteristically personalized in God who says "I AM that I AM."[15] In faith man realizes his creatureliness and his guilt and surrenders all his "boasting," all desire to live on his own resources. Faith is an unconditional response to the grace of God. It is through faith that man is saved. "Whatsoever is not of faith is sin," says St Paul.[16] The distinctive characteristic of the Biblical religions is not *knowledge* but *faith*.[17]

Above all, man the creature must realize his nothingness compared to the majesty of God. Although, according to the Biblical story, man was created in the image of God, he was soon expelled from the Garden of Eden for his disobedience in the act of eating the forbidden fruit of the tree of knowledge. "And the Lord God said, Behold, the man is become as one of us, to know good and evil: and now, lest he put forth his hand, and take also of the tree of life, and eat, and live for ever: Therefore the Lord God sent him forth from the Garden of Eden, to till the ground from whence he was taken. So he drove out the man."[18] The God of judgment punished, and would punish, all those who disobey Him. Disobedience is a breach of faith, for the primary meaning of faith, both in the Old and the New Testament, is *obedience*.[19] "This is the end of the matter: you have heard it all: Fear God and obey His commands; there is no more to man than this. For God brings everything we do to judgment, and every secret, whether good or bad."[20]

THE UNBRIDGEABLE GAP

The lesson is driven home again and again that man cannot and must not question the ways and motives of

God. We see this in the story of the Tower of Babel[21] and again in the story of Job. The unbridgeable gap between the power and majesty of God on the one hand and the impotence of man on the other is strikingly brought out in the Book of Job (Chapters 38-42): God challenges Job to answer, "Where wast thou when I laid the foundations of the earth, declare, if thou hast understanding. Canst thou lift up thy voice to the clouds, that abundance of waters may cover thee? Shall he that contendeth with the Almighty instruct him? He that reproveth God, let him answer it . . . . Job answered the Lord, and said, "Behold, I am vile, what shall I answer Thee . . . . I know that Thou canst do everything and that no thought can be withholden from Thee. I abhor myself, and repent in dust and ashes."

The Old Testament in particular affirms that man must know his proper place before God. "The voice said, cry. And he said, what shall I cry? All flesh is grass, and all the goodliness thereof as the flowers of the field: The grass withereth, the flower fadeth; but the word of our God shall stand forever."[22] As Kierkegaard says, "Before God man is always wrong."[23] One of the essential steps on the way to salvation is to recognize and submit to this great gulf between a human being and the Deity. Man cannot aspire to become like Him.[24] Indeed to attempt this is the greatest sin of all; this is the very essence of the devil. This is what Adam was tempted into trying, and he was punished. This is what Lucifer attempted, and he was expelled from heaven. Man cannot be saved by his own efforts; salvation comes from outside him, by the grace of God to whom, as St Paul says, one must "pray without ceasing."[25] Man must fear the God of redemption, who is *totaliter alter*, the Wholly Other, altogether perfect and outside, the only reality.

"The Father and I are one." When some of the
Jews again reached for rocks to stone him, Jesus
protested to them, "Many good deeds have I shown
you from the Father. For which of these do you
stone me?" "It is not for any 'good deed' that we are
stoning you," the Jews retorted, "but for blasphem-
ing. You who are only a man are making yourself
God."[26]

In spite of the teaching and example of Jesus Christ
himself, as we shall see later, very few, if any, elements
of that stream of spirituality which aims at union or
oneness with God have flourished in the Biblical tradition, which insists on the unbridgeable chasm
between man the creature and God the Creator.
Mysticism of any sort has been suspect, but more
especially when it is given a monistic interpretation,
that is, when the soul is said to become one with God.
This is particularly true of the pre-Christian Judaism
and the mainstream of Protestantism which are not
only unmystical but definitely anti-mystical.[27] The
creature man must never forget his total dependence
on God's grace, which comes unconditionally when it
may. This grace is not a reward for anything; it cannot
be forced or won by any effort whatsoever. It is a
totally undeserved and unearned blessing. "The
highest of human tasks," wrote Kierkegaard, "is for a
man to allow himself to be completely persuaded that
he can of himself do nothing, absolutely nothing."[28]

THE HOPE FOR SALVATION

"Now faith is the substance of things hoped for, the
evidence of things not seen."[29] What is hoped for is
redemption from sin and death. If we have faith in the
Lord, He will grant us eternal salvation. "God is our
refuge and strength," as the psalmist says, "a very

present help in trouble."[30] "Truly my soul waiteth
upon God: from Him cometh my salvation. My soul,
wait thou only upon God: for my expectation is from
Him. He only is my rock and my salvation: He is my
defence, I shall not be moved."[31] Hope is a dominant
note of the Bible, and one of St Paul's triumvirate of
graces.[32] In Judaism there was a lively hope that God
would deliver the nation from bondage and restore its
former glory. This hope fed upon the predictions of
salvation in the prophets and lived on in prayers and
hymns like the Psalms. Its classical expression is to be
found in the apocalyptic literature.[33] In its traditional
form, the hope of Israel was communal in character.
With Jesus, however, it became individual, resting on
the eschatological preaching, dealing with redemption and life after death. He believed that a new order
was close at hand and the time of decision was in the
present. "The time is fulfilled and the Reign of God
has drawn nigh."[34]

For many Christians the primary religious experience is not faith or love but *hope*: hope in the
Kingdom of God to come in the future or the afterlife.
Faith and hope are the dispositions of those who are
looking for the grace of God as a future possibility.
In this form, they are distinctively Judaeo-Christian
attitudes. Since man can do nothing on his own to save
himself, he puts his faith in the grace of God and hopes
for salvation. For this he has the promise of God's
prophet: "Then answered Peter and said unto him,
Behold we have forsaken all, and followed thee: what
shall we have therefore? and Jesus said unto them,
Verily I say unto you, that ye which have followed me,
in the regeneration when the Son of Man shall sit on
the throne of His Glory, ye also shall sit upon twelve
thrones, judging the twelve tribes of Israel. And everyone that hath forsaken houses, or brethren, or sisters,

or father, or mother, or wife, or children, or lands, for my name's sake, shall receive an hundredfold, and shall inherit everlasting life."[35]

Hope is what gives man strength in his faith. So does fear of punishment and eternal damnation. *Hope* and *fear* are metaphysical and psychological correlates of each other, as are *faith* and *doubt*. One invokes the other. One is always afraid that one may not obtain what one hopes for, and that one may not escape the "damnation of hell" to which the unbelievers are doomed.[36] As hope is sustained by God and heaven, so devil and hell emerge to maintain fear. It is not only faith and hope that are distinctively Judaeo-Christian religious attitudes, so are doubt and fear.

Loving Our Neighbors

The third grace in the triumvirate of St Paul is *charity*. "And now abideth faith, hope, charity, these three; but the greatest of these is charity."[37] We read in the Bible: "What doth it profit, my brethren, though a man say he hath faith, and have not works? Can faith save him? ... But wilt thou know, O vain man, that faith without works is dead."[38] While this is characteristic of the New Testament, one would search in vain in the entire Indian tradition for a scriptural passage underscoring the importance of charitable acts, for the benefit of the needy and the downtrodden, expressed so forcefully as:

Then the King will say to those at his right hand, 'Come, O blessed of my Father, inherit the kingdom prepared for you from the foundation of the world; for I was hungry and you gave me food, I was thirsty and you gave me drink, I was a stranger and you welcomed me, I was naked and you clothed me, I was sick and you visited me, I was in prison and you

came to me.' Then the righteous will answer him,
'Lord, when did we see thee hungry and feed thee,
or thirsty and give thee drink? And when did we
see thee a stranger and welcome thee, or naked and
clothe thee? And when did we see thee sick or in
prison and visit thee?' And the King will answer
them, 'Truly, I say to you, as you did it to one of the
least of these my brethren, you did it to me.'[39]

Modern translators of the Bible rightly render
agape, the third and the highest grace, as *love* rather
than *charity*, a word which for us moderns has come to
mean only benevolent or charitable acts. For St Paul
agape is obviously something much greater, as his
whole magnificent hymn to love indicates: "And
though I bestow all my goods to feed the poor, and
though I give my body to be burned, and have not love
(agape), it profiteth me nothing.... Love never faileth:
but whether there be prophecies, they shall fail;
whether there be tongues, they shall cease; whether
there be knowledge, it shall vanish away."[40]

To start with, God loves man. God loved the world so
much that He gave His "only begotten son."[41] To deliver mankind from sin, the Son of God, "who had
always been God by nature, did not cling to His pre-
rogative as God's equal, but stripped Himself of all
privileges by consenting to be a slave by nature and
being born as mortal man. And, having become man,
he humbled himself by living a life of utter obedience,
even to the extent of dying, and the death He died was
the death of a common criminal."[42] The Son of God
died to express His love, for "greater love hath no man
than this, that a man lay down his life for his friends."[43]

In return, God demands man's love for Him and
obedience to His laws. "And thou shalt love the Lord
thy God with all thy heart, and with all thy soul, and
with all thy might."[44] The love of God, which He

bestows, and the love of man, which He expects, correspond with each other. Sometimes it begins from
above: "because the Lord loved you, and because He
would keep the oath which He had sworn unto your
fathers . . ."[45] Sometimes it comes from below: "And
now, Israel, what doth the Lord thy God require of
thee, but to fear the Lord thy God, to walk in all His
ways, and to love Him and to serve Him . . ."[46] All else
that God requires from the faithful comes from this
one thing: because they love Him, they cleave to Him,
follow Him in His ways, hearken to His voice, keep His
commandments, and serve Him.[47] The Lord God
wants His people to be holy as He is holy, to be perfect
as He is perfect, to be merciful as He is merciful.[48]

"Master, which is the great commandment in the
law?" Jesus said unto him, "Thou shalt love the Lord
thy God with all thy heart, and with all thy soul, and
with all thy mind. This is the first and the great commandment. And the second is like unto it. Thou shalt
love thy neighbour as thyself. On these two commandments hang all the law and the prophets."[49] Nowhere
else in the writings of mankind has loving one's fellow
man been placed so unequivocally on the same level
as loving God; this commandment comprehends all
other ethical precepts. There is no longer any need for
formulated definitions, for we all know how we would
like others to treat us in a similar situation.

Nor is this emphasis on loving one's neighbor an
isolated one in the Judaeo-Christian tradition. We
read in Leviticus (19:18): "Thou shalt love thy neighbour as thyself." Hillel, at the end of the first century
B.C., is said to have been the author of the *Golden Rule*
summary of the Torah: "What is hateful to thee, do not
do to anyone else: this is the whole law and the rest is
commentary." Rabbi Akiba, a century later, summed
up the whole law in the saying: "Love thy neighbour

as thyself." We hear St Paul saying: ". . . for all the law is fulfilled in one word, even in this; Thou shalt love thy neighbour as thyself."[50] This commandment is so strongly stated that often it begins to appear to be the center of the whole tradition—even foreshadowing the commandment that precedes it in which man is asked to love God.

THE LOVE OF GOD

Ultimately, however, it is to God that we must return, for there is no salvation here below, no salvation anywhere or anyhow except through Him. As long as we live at the level of our lower nature, the sinful passions work in our bodies to bear fruit for death. It is only if we *repent* and turn to God that our sins can be wiped out.[51] The Greek word which is translated as *repentance* in the New Testament is *metanoia*; it literally means *change of mind*. Only if we change our mind and heart and reorient ourselves according to our spiritual nature can we hope for redemption from sin, suffering, and death. "I will tell you this: unless you turn round and become like children, you will never enter the Kingdom of Heaven."[52] As long as we are by ourselves, depending on our own resources, "bursting with the futile conceit of worldly minds," as St Paul says, we are in the hands of the evil one.[53] From him we can be delivered only if we put our faith and trust in God, the Holy One of Israel. "We know that so long as we are at home in the body we are exiles from the Lord," and unless we change our heart and repent, we shall perish.[54] But God's grace is lavished upon us when we sincerely seek Him.

Consider the lilies of the field, how they grow; they neither toil nor spin; yet I tell you, even Solomon in all his glory was not arrayed like one of these. But if God so clothes the grass of the field, which today is alive and tomorrow is thrown into the oven, will he not much more clothe you, O men of little faith? Therefore do not be anxious, saying, 'What shall we eat?' or 'What shall we drink?' or 'What shall we wear?' ... your heavenly Father knows that you need them all. But seek first his kingdom and his righteousness, and all these things shall be yours as well.[55]

5

The Parting of the Ways

Both the Judaeo-Christian and the Indian tradition start from the fact that man, as he is, is a very limited being, fragmented and not whole. Awareness of this fact marks the beginning of religious life. How strongly it seizes us determines how alienated we feel from the ordinary humanity around us and inside us—with its useless preoccupation with acquisition and performance. This alienation—this feeling of being "a stranger"[1]—is what delineates the spiritual problem: authentic living in the face of this estrangement, waking up from the dead, coming to be. In this lies the quest for meaning and purpose in human life. From alienation to meaning—this is the beginning of the movement from sin to salvation, from bondage to freedom.

The fundamental human limitation is that of time. There will be a time when we shall not be any more. Children of Chronos, we shall be devoured by him.

Awareness of this dissolution of self is the source of all metaphysical anxiety.

> Nor dread, nor hope attend
> A dying animal;
> A man awaits his end
> Dreading and hoping all.
> W. B. Yeats

The inevitable and irreducible fact of death has impressed itself upon us with great force since the earliest times. For some, like Plato, the entire philosophic life is a life of constant preparation for death. The arbitrariness of the time when we might be struck down by death increases the poignancy of the situation. We are like a prisoner condemned to death, except that he does not know which hour will signal his execution. "What is life for? To die? To kill myself at once? No, I am afraid. To wait for death till it comes? I fear that even more. Then I must live. But what for? In order to die? And I could not escape from that circle."[2]

No one can escape from that circle—except one who looks at both life and death alike, from a higher consciousness. At our ordinary level of consciousness, in our usual situation of sleep, what we call *life* and what we call *death* are opposed to each other; we run from the one and seek the other. We cling to life, busying ourselves with weighty things, hoping to deny our mortality. The greatest wonder, according to the *Mahabharata*, is that even when we see people around us dying, no one is really convinced that he himself will die.

To be aware of the human condition is to be aware of man's limitations; it is to see oneself as a dying animal. This is the source of existential *angst*. As

Sartre says, "Man is anguish," and Yeats writes, "We have not begun to live until we conceive life as a tragedy." St Augustine speaks of "the ceaseless unrest that marks the temporal life of the individual."[3] *Angst* is the overwhelming feeling that somehow, something is radically wrong in man's relation with the cosmos. This is what the Christian means when he says that man is *sinful*: "The whole world lieth in wickedness."[4]

For the Buddha, the first of the Four Noble Truths was: there is sorrow (*dukkha*, suffering). The whole thought of India is so utterly permeated by this fact of human bondage—inextricably connected with the very fact of being born—that the entire culture seems to be obsessed with an existential anguish.[5] This obsession of India is equalled by the obsession of the Judaeo-Christian tradition with the nothingness of man. From the point of view of an individual, however, both of these amount to the same thing—man finds himself not whole in a broken world in which he is trapped. That it is expressed differently in the two traditions is very significant and has far-reaching consequences.

THE WAY OUT

In the face of the anguish inherent in the human condition, we meet an overwhelming desire for salvation from sin, for deliverance from sorrow, for freedom from bondage. St Paul says, "O wretched man that I am! Who shall deliver me from this body of death?"[6] The suffering individual cries out in the words of the *Upanishad*:

> Lead me from the unreal to the real,
> Lead me from darkness to light,
> Lead me from death to immortality.[7]

When Siddhartha, the young Buddha saw three sights —an old man, a diseased man, and a dead man—he was so struck by the presence of suffering in human life that his desire for learning the cause and cessation of suffering caused him to renounce the world—his wife, son, palace, kingdom—in order to search for enlightenment.

The possibility of moving from the worldly darkness to spiritual light is essential to religion. And this movement constitutes its total essence. For a spiritual life, rituals, images, idols, churches, scriptures, and ideas about God may all be irrelevant; they may or may not be helpful. It appears that at some stage in his spiritual evolution, an awakening individual has to go beyond all these symbols, dogmas, and words, even if this incurs the wrath of established ecclesiastical authority. This is why intensely spiritual people often have not been tolerated by organized religions.

Of course, it is possible to deny that there is a way out of man's suffering. That,in fact, is the prevailing mood in the contemporary philosophy on the European continent. Sartre summarized this attitude by saying, "L'homme est une passion inutile (Man is a futile passion)."[8] Neither the Judaeo-Christian nor the Indian tradition subscribes to this position for they believe that there is salvation for man. But, how this salvation is to be achieved and what it consists of are generally expressed differently. However, they both agree not only that man, by his very existence, is sinful or is in bondage, but also that this state of affairs comes about because man gives his little self, his ego, an undue importance—without consideration of its place in the cosmic whole.

Some Zen students do not realize the true man in a mask.

Because they recognize ego-soul!
Ego-soul is the seed of birth and death,
And foolish people call it the true man.[9]

Why does man do this? The Jews and the Christians
reply that it is because he is fallen from grace owing
to Original Sin.[10] The Indian would say it is because of
ignorance. But the task for both is the same: to free
man from the shackles of his little ego so that he may
be born again in the Spirit. They both see man in this
life as a "stranger and a pilgrim," as a "sojourner,"
as a "wayfarer," who has "no continuing city but seeks
one to come... which hath foundations, whose builder
and maker is God."[11] Man is a pilgrim between his
ordinary existence and his true existence, his authentic being. His ego, his little will, stands in his way.

I came out alone on my way to my tryst. But who is
this that follows me in the silent dark?
I move aside to avoid his presence but I escape
him not.
He makes the dust rise from the earth with his
swagger; he adds his loud voice to every word that
I utter.
He is my own little self, my lord, he knows no shame;
but I am ashamed to come to thy door in his
company.[12]

Rabindranath Tagore

The Judaeo-Christian tradition teaches that the
way out of his dilemma is by faith, for, as St Paul says,
all that "is not of faith is sin."[13] In faith man realizes his
creatureliness and guilt, the impotence of his will, and
his nothingness. This faith is not in any object or any
principle but in the Living Person, in God, who
responds. Or, rather, who calls—for man to respond.
To this Holy One, full of mercy, one surrenders

oneself. "Not what I will, but what Thou wilt."[14]

> Two men went up into the temple to pray; the one a
> Pharisee, and the other a publican. The Pharisee
> stood and prayed thus with himself, God, I thank
> Thee that I am not as other men are, extortioners,
> unjust, adulterers, or even as this publican. I fast
> twice in the week, I give tithes of all that I possess.
> And the publican, standing afar off, would not lift
> up so much as his eyes unto heaven, but smote
> upon his breast, saying, God, be merciful unto me a
> sinner. I tell you this man went down to his house
> justified rather than the other: for everyone that
> exalteth himself shall be abased; and he that
> humbleth himself shall be exalted.[15]

The great German mystic, Boehme, said, "Thou
shalt do nothing but forsake thy own will, viz., that
which thou callest 'I' or 'Thyself.' By which all thy evil
properties will grow weak, faint and ready to die; and
then thou wilt sink down again into that one thing,
from which thou art originally sprung."[16]

According to the Indian tradition, however, the way
out of man's suffering is to overcome the ignorance
which is the cause of suffering. Freedom is obtained
through knowledge of one's authentic self, one's true
being, one's Atman, the Person behind the mask of ego
and personality. Become what you really are, for
ultimately you are Brahman; it is only when deceived
by ignorance that you feel sundered and afflicted. The
Buddha said, "Look within, thou art the Buddha."[17]
With this discovery, the mystic-poet shouts with joy:

> I have discovered my deep breathless being:
> 　Masked by front of mind, immense, serene,
> It meets the world with an Immortal's seeing,
> 　A god-spectator of the human scene.[18]
> Aurobindo

Freedom does not have its abode in some special place or heaven where we arrive after we are dead. "Freedom is not in a particular place nor has one to go to some other village in order to obtain it," says a scripture. "The destruction of the knot of ignorance round our hearts is known as freedom."[19] One must search for deliverance while alive, in this very body, and not merely hope for it after death.

> If your bonds be not broken whilst living, what hope of deliverance in death?
> It is but an empty dream, that the soul shall have union with Him because it has passed from the body:
> If He is found now, He is found then,
> If not, we do but go to dwell in the City of Death.[20]

I AM BRAHMAN

The liberating knowledge, as understood in the spiritual tradition of India, does not mean sensual or rational knowledge. "It is not the knowledge of the senses, nor is it relative knowledge, nor yet inferential knowledge. Beyond the senses, beyond the understanding, beyond all expression is *turiya* (the fourth state of consciousness)."[21] The *Upanishads* distinguish between lower knowledge and higher knowledge. The former gives us the knowledge of the scriptures and the sciences, whereas the latter is "that by which the Undecaying is apprehended."[22] According to the *Katha Upanishad* (I.2:12), the Self is perceived not by logical reason but by spiritual contemplation. The Buddha said, "Through meditation wisdom is won, through lack of meditation wisdom is lost: let a man who knows this double path of gain and loss so conduct himself that wisdom may grow."[23]

Obviously, this path of contemplation is neither possible nor suitable for everyone. Mankind consists of a variety of temperaments; it is only natural that different people should choose different paths. Since men are different, their needs, desires, questions, and capacities differ. In the Indian tradition, there are four major yogas, paths to union with Brahman; each person chooses a combination of these four which is suitable for himself. The four paths are: the path of knowledge (*jnana yoga*), path through meditation and psychic control (*dhyana yoga*), path of love and devotion (*bhakti yoga*), and the path of union through works (*karma yoga*). Naturally, these paths are not exclusive of each other: emphasis on one at a given time for a particular person depends on his level of development and specific need. At the level of manifestation there is a great relativism in India: literally thousands of gods, symbols, ideas, idols, and images are available. One can start with any one of them that corresponds to his need and type. The question is not whether any particular ideas or gods are true or false, since knowledge—and therefore the truth or falsity—depends upon the level and state of one's consciousness. Rather, the question is whether these ideas, gods, or practices are adequate (or inadequate) for the person involved and the end he has in mind. As a person changes, what he needs and finds adequate also changes. The ultimate end in India is the state of integration, samadhi, the highest state of consciousness in which alone the Atman is apprehended. Elaborate external worship and ritual has been developed by religions in India, particularly by those believing predominantly in *bhakti yoga* (like the devotees of Vishnu, or Shiva or Devi, the mother goddess). But all Indian religion conceives Brahman to be the innermost core of an individual.[24]

This, as we have already seen, is central to the Indian tradition: liberation is within oneself and consists in becoming what one truly is. There is a total inwardness in the goal set for man. The Person that we must seek, knowing whom alone the knot of ignorance is destroyed, is within ourselves. This is very different from the mainstream of the Judaeo-Christian tradition in which the Person one hopes for, God, is outside us. Redemption can come only from the outside and not from within, however deeply we delve into ourselves. In fact, the greatest of all sins is to believe that man by himself can do anything, let alone save himself. Only God can save man, and in attempting to be his own savior, man is repeating the Fall. This is the gravest of all sins.

Contrasted with the Judaeo-Christian insistence on the nothingness of man is the Indian insistence on the everythingness of man. This central difference can be brought into a sharper focus by considering the strict non-dualistic position of the *Advaita Vedanta*, which has exponents from the sages of the *Upanishads* to Raman Maharishi in our own time. According to this perspective, in the highest state of samadhi, knower and known become one, object and subject lose their distinction, and the yogi exclaims: "I am Brahman . . . I do not require any special condition or proof to know that my name is Devdatta. Similarly, for a knower of Brahman, the knowledge that I am Brahman does not require any proof."[25] This expression of non-dualism is naturally, philosophically disputable. In India the famous saint Ramanuja opposed it vigorously. The dispute is centered on the precise nature of the relation between the innermost self of man, Atman, and the Universal Self, Brahman. Whatever be the truth—if the truth of these depths can be expressed in language at all—to the inward-looking

Indian tradition, the expression "I am Brahman" is one of the four *great utterances* of the sages representing the quintessence of the whole culture.[26] According to a very important stream of the Indian spirituality, to know Brahman is to become Brahman, and deliverance consists in becoming one with Brahman.[27]

Such teachings are not unknown in the West. For example, Plotinus asserts that to *know* the One, by a kind of superrational insight, means to become one with it, which the soul can accomplish by becoming as simple or as *alone* as the One. In the moment of such union, the soul has become God, or rather is God.[28] Nevertheless, to the Jews this claim of oneness with God was the highest of blasphemies, and their main charge against Jesus Christ. The Christian reaction to this monism is illuminating: "The mystic who triumphantly realizes his essential oneness with God, or with the World-Order, or the Divine, knowing himself in serene equanimity the supreme master of the universe and his own destiny, and who by marvelous feats of moral self-restraint offers a fascinating example of splendid humanity, nevertheless, in the light of Biblical revelation, commits in this sublime way the root-sin of mankind—'to be like God.' In other words: *he repeats the Fall.* In India, for instance, the part of divine reality and truth which has, owing to the initiative of the self-disclosing God, succeeded in shining through to man, is all . . . inevitably vitiated by this monistic tendency, which is regarded as the pride, not as the avowed stumbling block, of India."[29]

MYSTICISM IN THE WEST

Meister Eckhart (1260-1328 A.D.), the great German Dominican mystic, of all the Christians is considered to be the closest to the monastic mystics of Vedanta.

He says, for example, "The knower and the known are one. Simple people imagine that they should see God, as if He stood there and they here. This is not so. God and I, we are one in knowledge."[30] In his classic study of Eckhart and the great Vedanta philosopher Shankara, Rudolph Otto writes: "To have or rather to be the one, undivided, eternal, imperishable *Brahman*, which is wholly Being, wholly Spirit, utter Joy, that alone, and that entirely—this is also the thirst and pride of the Indian seeker after salvation. There can be no doubt that this is also its meaning for Eckhart and that it differs fundamentally and essentially from the simpler Christian conception of salvation, to which it must always seem an extravagance, a Titanic pride, and an impossible transgression of the limitations of the creature—a 'Faustian urge,' as we call it today."[31]

The monistic mystical experience, in which there is a complete identity between the deepest part of the soul and God, although not unique to India, has not been encouraged or even tolerated in the Judaeo-Christian tradition or in Islam. It is difficult to think of even a single example in the entire history of the Biblical religions when a monistic mystic was accepted without qualification. In spite of some obviously mystical sayings of Jesus, such as his prayer, ". . . May they all be one: as thou, Father, art in me, and I in thee, so also may they be one in us,"[32] such monism has been put down quite severely in Christianity. Those who believed in such doctrines were often cast out as heretics, and their writings were destroyed. Erigena was condemned for his doctrine of pantheistic mysticism; so were the Brethren of the Free Spirit who developed the creed that "the Christian must seek to become like God. If man turns from external to inward things, lets God be God, then he will resemble God, will be God and will no longer need God." Eckhart's works were condemned by the Church and are still under a ban; the stigma of heresy is attached to him even now.[33]

Mysticism of any kind is essentially a product of an inward-looking contemplative attitude, and it has been generally absent from the mainstream of the Judaeo-Christian tradition, whereas in India this is accepted as the ultimate crowning glory of a man's spiritual efforts. Sometimes a distinction is made between monistic and monotheistic mysticism, with an eye to establishing the superiority of one or the other.[34] Examples of both kinds abound in India, whereas in Biblical religions, whenever mysticism asserts itself at all—as in some Christian medieval mystics, and Sufism in Islam—it is usually of a monotheistic kind, in which the One God remains ultimately over and above even the deepest part of human soul. It is doubtful that these two kinds of experiences are essentially different from each other—except in the linguistic-theological interpretations placed on them, either by the mystics themselves or by others.[35] In any event, both Judaism and Christianity, in particular Protestantism, look upon mysticism of any sort with suspicion. Some authors have gone so far as to suggest that mysticism may be one of the subtlest enemies of Christianity.[36] Perhaps the major reason for the relative lack of mysticism in the Biblical tradition is the belief in the transcendent holiness and majesty of God and man's nothingness in the face of Him. Even otherwise, mysticism cannot be very acceptable in the doctrines firmly based on some unique past events—as is the case for all the three Biblical religions—Judaism, Christianity and Islam—for, above all, a mystic believes in salvation through the present life of the spirit in man and an inner recurrence of the past redemptive deeds. For him it is the present suffering of the inner Christ which brings salvation rather than the death of the historical Jesus.

PROPHETISM

The characteristic spiritual experience in the Biblical religions is not mysticism but prophetism.[37] India has no prophets like Moses, Isaiah, Jeremiah, Jesus, or Mohammed—those who are chosen by God to speak on His behalf and to do His bidding. All the prophets are commanded by God to reveal His message to the entire community of believers, or to the whole of Israel. The revelation of God is not for the sake of one individual. In general, the prophetic utterances concern the moral and social failings of the community which must repent and mend its ways, and act in accordance with the expressed will and commandments of God. Otherwise, the community will be punished by God, and each person singly, either right away or by damnation to hell after death. The sages of India—from the most ancient times to the contemporary—exude an entirely different feeling. Whether one looks at the ancient sages (like Yajnavalkya, Vyasa, Kapila, Patanjali or the Buddha) or the modern ones (like Ramakrishna, Raman, Aurobindo, and Krishnamurti) one finds a very different quality of energy. The Indian sages display a finer and subtler quality of feeling, not the vigorous and robust energy of the Biblical prophets. The prophetic emphasis seems to be always on action and obedience to the will of God rather than on the deepening of insight; on reform rather than understanding. The Indian sages, on the other hand, stress the inner vision and the transcendent wisdom from which the right action naturally follows, as fragrance from a flower.

It is worth remarking that the case of Jesus Christ is somewhat unique in this regard, sharing pronounced characteristics of both the prophetic and the mystical types. We must take into account the Hellenized background of the Jewish community at the time of Jesus Christ, the fact that the Gospels were written down in Greek rather than in Hebrew, and the profound similarities between some schools of Indian thought and of Greek philosophy. Also, the possibility of Brahmanic and Buddhist influences on some Greek thinkers, particularly the Gnostic and Neo-Platonic, can by no means be ruled out. It is interesting that precisely in those Gospels which have been influenced by these latter currents of thought—such as the Gospel According to St John and the Gospel According to St Thomas—one encounters the most mystical sayings of Jesus Christ, who comes through as a combination of a upanishadic mystic-sage and an incarnation (*avatara*) of Vishnu who descends for the sake of the world whenever there is need.

AVATARS

These avatars descend from above in animal, human, or hybrid form, whatever is necessary. Nine such incarnations of Vishnu, the preserver aspect of the Divine, are supposed to have already taken place during the present cycle of the universe, one Day of Brahma, which will last 4,320,000,000 human years. Supreme among these incarnations was Krishna who delivered the message of the *Bhagavad Gita*. He declared there: "Wherever there is decline of righteousness (*dharma*) and the rise of unrighteousness, O Bharata, then I send forth (incarnate) myself. For the protection of the good, for the destruction of the wicked and for the establishment of righteousness,

I come into being from age to age."[38]

Evil as such is never completely destroyed by Vishnu, for that would eliminate the counterplay between godlike and demonic, productive and destructive energies. For the continuation and maintenance of the world, both "good" and "evil" are required; the *avatars* only set their balance aright.

This principle is illustrated in myths. For example, the mighty serpent Kaliya lodged himself in the Yamuna river, thus spreading his poison and causing tremendous suffering and death to the human beings and animals of the region. Finally, seeing the agony of all the beings, Krishna jumped into the river in order to subdue Kaliya. After a great struggle, the thousand-headed serpent was overpowered and Krishna was dancing on his head in order to kill him. The consorts of Kaliya, that is to say, his many powers, emerged from the river to plead with Krishna to spare the life of the serpent, for after all he was simply fulfilling his serpent *dharma*, his proper function and calling, by spreading poison. Even the serpent was created by the same divine power which created the other animals, each with his specific dharma. Krishna, as the upholder of dharma, at all levels, accepted their plea. He suggested, however, that Kaliya was carrying out his dharma at the wrong place, and banished him to the ocean where his poison could be contained.[39]

Inevitably, however, the forces of order and those of disorder will again get out of proper proportion, and again Vishnu will incarnate himself. Thus this play of the Lord, this cosmos, will forever continue to undergo successive cycles of creation and destruction. "Life in the cycle of the countless rebirths is like a vision in a dream. The gods on high, the mute trees and the stones, are alike apparitions in this phantasy. But Death administers the law of time. Ordained by time,

Death is the master of all. Perishable as bubbles are the good and the evil of the beings of the dream. In unending cycles the good and evil alternate. Hence, the wise are attached to neither, neither the evil nor the good. The wise are not attached to anything at all."[40]

According to this cyclical nature of time, endless avatars will appear in the endless number of universes. Thus Krishna becomes a mythic figure, not only connected with some particular fact or specific chronological time.[41] He does not come to herald a golden age which will last forever. The serpent cycle of time will go on revolving through ascending and descending periods everlastingly, without pause and without mercy. The cosmic dance of Shiva will continue, different steps marking creation and destruction of the worlds. This is in pronounced contrast to the Judaeo-Christian teleological evaluation of time, according to which the world is progressing towards perfection under the direction of God. The well known hymn succinctly characterizes it: "God is working his purpose out, as year succeeds to year."

HISTORY AND PROGRESS

Yehweh made His covenant with Abraham at a particular historical time, and the hopes of Jews were bound up with the fulfillment of this covenant in the future. Hebrew philosophy of history comprehends the whole course of time, from the very moment of the world's creation to its final apocalyptic end, and the whole vast panorama of events is seen as the gradual unfolding of God's purpose, namely, the final triumph of His chosen people, Israel.[42] Perhaps the most important single legacy passed on by Judaism to Christianity was this conviction that the course of

historical events has a profound significance. This no
doubt has been of immense importance in the development of worldly sciences and social institutions
in Christian countries. Time here is viewed completely linearly; temporal events move in a linear
progression towards their completion in eternity. In
Tennyson's words, we find a classic expression of this
view:

> One God, one law, one element
> And one far-off divine event,
> To which the whole creation moves.[43]

The key events in the history of the world, the major
cosmic moments, are unique in the Judaeo-Christian
view of time. The world was created at a definite
time; Jesus was born, crucified, and resurrected at
specific historical moments—unique and momentous.
The uniqueness of these events, particularly of the
Incarnation, required a belief that history is a straight
line sequence guided by God.[44] Pagan belief in pur-
poseless temporal undulation was entirely unacceptable to early Christians. The idea of the cosmic
repetitive cycles was the worst of blasphemies. Origen
argued in the third century that from such a theory it
follows that "Adam and Eve will do once more exactly
what they have already done; the same deluge will be
repeated; the same Moses will bring the same six
hundred thousand people out of Egypt; Judas will
again betray his Lord; and Paul a second time will hold
the coats of those who stone Stephen." "God forbid,"
cried St Augustine in the next century "that we
should believe this. For Christ died once for our sins,
and rising again, dies no more."[45] Thus, with the rise of
Christianity, the prevalent doctrines of undulation
and recurrent cycles vanished from the Mediterranean

world. No more radical revolution has ever taken place in the world-outlook of a large area. Along with the uniqueness of the key events and linearity of time, the Judaeo-Christian world-view is permeated with the thought that history is going somewhere. There is no antagonism here between time and God. God rules over history and works His plan out in time. Both in the history of the Church and in the life of an individual, the divine purpose is still being worked out. Ultimately, this divine purpose would reach its culmination, and Christ would return, the dead would be raised, and the final judgment enacted, with eternal beatitude for the saved and eternal punishment for the damned.[46]

SALVATION FROM ABOVE OR WITHIN?

In the Biblical tradition, the idea of God being incarnated in animal form is totally abhorrent. Even the idea of human incarnation is quite blasphemous in Judaism and Islam. In Christianity, of course, the single exception is Jesus Christ himself who was "the only begotten son of God" and His equal.[47] Jesus Christ was declared by the great Church councils to be fully divine and fully human. No one else, however exalted, can be accepted to be divine. Thus, in spite of the many obviously mystical sayings of Jesus, the mainstream of Christianity interprets his message in the manner of the prophetic tradition, with its orientation to God who is essentially different from all others. Man is here, and God there; He is totally transcendent, both in thought and experience. The prophetic tradition does not accept a continuous scale of being along which there is a vertical movement. Rather, there is a radical discontinuity between the animal and the human, and, more importantly, between the human and the divine. Any attempt to transgress our humanity is futile and sinful.

In general, the Indian sage seeks and finds his enlightenment within himself, whereas the Biblical prophets are sought by God who reveals His commandments to them. The sacred moments in which the inner core of man's soul communes with the Ultimate Reality are interpreted differently in the two traditions. These may be two radically different experiences, indicating a basic dimorphism in the human psyche. Or, perhaps, these are different interpretations—owing to different languages and cultures—of the same basic encounter. It is possible that at the primary spiritual level the two types of experiences are essentially the same. It should be mentioned that the great Jewish philosopher Philo (30 B.C. - 50 A.D.)—perhaps owing to the Greek influence— interpreted the prophetic experience in terms of mystical ecstasy.

In either case, very different concepts of religions and associated terminologies have emerged from this contrast between two kinds of experiences, or two kinds of interpretations of similar experience. In one we have *sin, faith, prayer, revelation, grace,* and *salvation.* These are the key words in the Judaeo-Christian corpus of redemptive literature and form the axis of the whole tradition. All these words, without exception, sound odd in the Hindu-Buddhist context, the hub of which is indicated by other words and ideas: *ignorance-illusion (avidya, maya), knowledge (jnana), practice-perfecting (sadhana), meditation (yoga), synthesis-integration (samadhi), illumination (bodhi),* and *liberation (moksha).*

In the Judaeo-Christian tradition the hope of salvation is from outside man, from God who is an external absolute and the ultimate authority. Human faith depends on the historical revelation of God through his specially chosen spokesmen. Encounter of an individual with God in the Biblical tradition is mediated, directly or indirectly, by His prophets, by His Word, or by His Church. Any immediate experience is therefore somehow always suspect, for immediacy by its very nature is indifferent to scriptural interpretations, organizational structures, or rational argumentation. These latter tend to constrict reality by insisting that the one true God has expressed Himself through one true Word and one true Church. Hence, in the extreme, we find excommunication of deviant believers, condemnation of unacceptable writings, burning of heretics, damnation of heathens. All of these persecutions are a burden peculiarly of the history of the Biblical religions. However, this becomes intelligible once we recognize the radical metaphysical dualism—between God and man, spirit and flesh, good and evil—that permeates the mainstream of the prophetic tradition. It is this dualism which is ultimately responsible for the dichotomous thinking which has so enthralled Western thought for centuries. Only an atomistic ego, sundered and isolated from the rest of the universe, can take seriously many of the "problems" to which philosophers have devoted so much attention: How is it possible to know the world, to understand other minds, or to comprehend God? There are persistent tensions in Western society: between humanism and theology, between the individual and the cosmos, between the outer world of scientific facts and the inner world of spiritual values, between time and eternity, between this shore and the other. Rarely have these been resolved into a creative synthesis, particularly in the modern period since the rise of science, Protestantism, capitalism, and individualism. Reduced to a single level, these aspects appear to be engaged in a direct either-or combat in which success of one necessarily means defeat of the other.

In the Indian tradition, on the other hand, deliverance is from within, from the innermost core of one's individuality, the core which is the same for all beings. Ultimately, there is no room for a metaphysical dualism here. For the Indian, gods and demons are all inside him, or rather they *are* him. What he seeks is neither inner nor outer, neither subjective nor objective, neither good nor evil. It is something beyond all these dichotomies and contradictions. There is no external absolute, and the final authority is in the Atman, which though within him is not the ego-self of man. However sacred the writings or any other authority, ultimately it is one's own deepest experience that counts. "When the awakening takes place" says Shankara, "scripture ceases to be authoritative."[48] The risk is, of course, of total relativization of, and often an indiscriminate acceptance of, innumerable gods, sects, and cults; no revelation in space and time is, from this point of view, ultimately any better than another. Thus, at the popular level mundane history as such, indeed the whole world of space-time, loses significance: after all, it is all a play of maya, the cosmic seductress; one must attempt to escape from this enchanting trap, for freedom is not in the world of names and forms.[49] For a common Indian, truth tends to become essentially a *personal* matter—not only in the sense that it is a subjective experience, but also that truth, whatever it may be, must express itself through a living person who is more often than not deified and worshipped. Thus, it becomes important to seek after gurus, wise or not so wise, rather than to seek objective facts about the world or even about oneself.

We must not forget that every tradition has its integrity; it is of a piece. The best insights of the sages and saints of a tradition have a discernible continuity with the worst misunderstandings and perversions of those insights by the mass of the people. This comes about through merciless workings of time, mechanicality, and quantity. The best and the worst of a culture are related to each other, almost as if one cannot exist without the other, except for short times or for small groups of people. The maintenance and continuation of any great truth or vision need such largeness of heart and soul and such sustained self-sacrifice that the general populace cannot be up to it, except under strict guidance from the spiritual elite of a community. Common understandings of the great spiritual principles in any religious tradition, precisely because they are common, are unreliable. Mass understandings are only on the surface; they cannot bespeak the depths.

Two Divergent Mainstreams

The great gulf between the two streams begins right at the beginning—or at least very close to it. Whatever the actual historical beginnings of their sources, the two traditions soon acquired very different starting points as far as an individual in the tradition is concerned, as he begins to be aware of himself and the world around him. Simply stated, the two starting points are: Man and God. In India, all spiritual concern centers on the individual person; he finds himself in bondage or in sorrow, not only as his personal problem but as a mark of existence comprising compelled and compulsive action (karma), from which he struggles to be free by self-realization. "I tell you this, the secret of the *Brahman*: there is nothing higher than man," declares the *Mahabharata*[50] There are aids, guide-posts, pathmarkers, teachers, but there are no saviors. "Work out your own salvation with diligence," said the Buddha. In the Biblical tradition, on the other hand, the starting point is God who is the active agent. He calls man to respond to the challenge of His revelation through His prophets. When an individual becomes aware of himself, he realizes how short he has fallen of what is expected of him by God, how sinful he is. Man's awareness of himself is through God's revelation. Man by himself is nothing; his salvation consists in the recognition of this fact and his total surrender to the will and grace of God, "for by grace are ye saved through faith; and that not of yourselves; it is the gift of God; not of works, lest any man should boast."[51]

So, St Paul says, "You . . . must be obedient . . . You must work out your own salvation in fear and trembling; for it is God who works in you, inspiring both the will and the deed, for his own chosen purpose."[52]

The Judaeo-Christian man is very confident of the grace of God to whose protection he can abandon himself like a child into the care of his mother.

> The Lord is my shepherd; I shall not want.
> He maketh me to lie down in green pastures;
> He leadeth me beside the still waters.
> He restoreth my soul: He leadeth me in the
> paths of righteousness for his name's sake.
> Yea, though I walk through the valley of
> the shadow of death, I will fear no evil; for
> thou art with me, thy rod and thy staff they
> comfort me.
> . . . . .
> Surely goodness and mercy will follow me
> all the days of my life; and I will dwell
> in the house of the Lord forever.[53]

Contrast this with the tale which was mentioned in the first chapter. The Indian believes that the great magician of maya has hypnotized man into thinking that his mask of personality is his true being and that he can abandon himself to the hands of the magician who is a good master. If man were to awaken from this deceitful hypnosis, he would realize the real horror of his existence in which, like a sheep, he is being led to the slaughter house. Then he would want to escape from the magician. If he can overcome the trance of illusion in which he is enveloped, he will realize his true self—which is not sheep at all—and the magician will no longer have any power over him.[54]

Clearly, each of the two traditions is very vast; an immense variety of people, ideas, and practices belong to each. It may even be true that everything that exists in one tradition can be found, in one form or another, in the other as well. Nevertheless, the mainstreams of the two traditions are very different at the societal, philosophical, and theological level. As an individual begins to struggle with his cultural conditioning, it is precisely the mainstream ideas and influences from which he needs to be liberated, so that he is freer to move towards the profounder wellspring of the tradition as well as of himself. An awareness of another tradition, which does not look at the human situation and possibilities in the same way as our own, can free us for a fresh look at the situation. In the process, we may come to question and understand the very nature of looking—whether veiled by conditioning or freshly —and being—either on the surface or at depth.

Some of the major differences in the mainstreams of the two traditions can be summarized as follows:

Aspect	Judaeo-Christian Tradition	Indian Tradition
Starting Point	God who calls (man, nation, community, Israel, Church)	Man who seeks (Self, God, Nirvana, Truth, Liberation)
Human Situation	Man is sinful	Man is in sorrow, in bondage
Cause of the present situation	Original Sin, disobedience to God's commandments	Craving, ignorance, illusion
Goal	Grace, salvation, heaven, everlasting life	Self-realization, enlightenment, liberation, freedom from everlasting life and death
Means	Repentance, faith, obedience, prayer, church	Self-study, knowledge, meditation, integration, individual effort, guru
Some characteristics	One God, one way, one savior (others are false, wrong, or inadequate)	One Truth, but necessarily many different ways to it
	God and Devil outside man	God and Devil within man
	Man is ultimately an unique individual	Ultimately there are no others; individuality is superficial
	Man and God are radically different	Man and God are radically one
	Man must realize his nothingness before God	Man must realize that all there is is Brahman, and he is Brahman.

Though they face the same human condition, the mainstreams of the Biblical and the Indian traditions seem to diverge immensely. Their formulations, images, symbols, parables, and legends appear so different. The essential difference between the two traditions is best brought out in the words of their most illustrious representatives, spoken to their favorite disciples. Christ asked Simon, "Who do you say I am?" He answered, "You are the Messiah, the Son of the Living God." Then Jesus said, "Simon, son of Jonah, you are favoured indeed! You did not learn that from mortal man; it was revealed to you by my heavenly Father. And I say this to you: You are Peter, the Rock; and on this rock I will build my church, and the powers of death shall never conquer it. I will give you the keys of the kingdom of Heaven; what you forbid on earth shall be forbidden in heaven, and what you allow on earth shall be allowed in heaven."[55] The Buddha, on the other hand, said, "Ananda, be ye lamps unto yourselves. Be a refuge to yourselves. Betake yourselves to no external refuge. Hold fast to the truth as a lamp. Hold fast as a refuge to the truth."[56]

6

From the Alone to the Alone

On the slopes of the mighty mountain there are many villages, each with its own deity and its own council responsible for the forms of worship and praise for the One who inhabits the mountaintop. Every few years, representatives from all the councils gather together to decide which slope is the best for the ascent. They all bring evidence and quote authorities, quarrel, and leave. Many move away from the slopes altogether and settle in the plains, some cherishing memories of the stories told by their forefathers after their climb. A few children hear the call from the top, amidst the din of worshippers in the temples and scholars in the councils. Only some of them have the strength and courage to undertake the long and arduous journey leading to the presence of the One who calls.

Who is it that calls us? How can we hear and respond? Is the source of the call inside us or above us?

"He who calls you is to be trusted," as St Paul says.[1] If we can find a way to attend to and trust this voice, we can leave theorizing aside and begin to learn to respond to the call. If we can keep our central question in mind, we are not likely to distract ourselves by arguments with our neighbor or attempts to convert him. Our need is for some practical way that will help us to be in our *right mind*—by which alone can we hear and see rightly. Until we develop an inner organ of discernment, we are without anchor, drifting with any chance wind.

SELF-KNOWLEDGE

In one of the Dialogues between *Disciple* and *Master*, Jacob Boehme wrote as follows:

> *The Disciple* said to his master: How may I come to the supersensual life, that I may see God and hear him speak? His *Master* said: When you can throw yourself but for a moment into that where no creature dwells, then you hear what God speaks.
>
> *Disciple:* Is that near at hand or far off?
>
> *Master:* It is within you and if you can for a while but cease from all your thinking and willing, then you shall hear the unspeakable words of God.[2]

In saying "It is within you" Boehme expressed an eternal truth which has been uttered by practically all the great teachers of the past. Christ said, "The Kingdom of God is within you."[3] Self-realization is the main theme of all the *Upanishads*. "He who knows that which is set in the secret place of the heart, he here on earth, O beloved, cuts asunder the knot of ignorance."[4]

However, this hidden one is not easily assigned a place. In a deep experience of listening or seeing, what is outside us is also inside. We ourselves are as mysterious as the kingdom and may hold the keys to it. If we can open the doors of the interior castle, the king might come and sit on the throne.

Self-knowledge is a prerequisite to, if not synonymous with, theology. According to Plutarch, the inscription at Delphi, "know thyself," is an injunction addressed by God to all who approach Him.[5] Man sees "the nature of *Brahman* through the nature of his own self, as by a lamp," says a *Upanishad*.[6] Plotinus said, "One that seeks to penetrate the nature of the Divine Mind must see deeply into the nature of his own soul, into the Divinest part of himself."[7] In fact, it appears that the only way to God is by self-knowing, dying to one's superficial self, and being born to a deeper self. There are clearly differences in detail and emphasis, but there is no other point on which there is a greater unanimity of principle among the various masters of spiritual becoming. One of the non-canonical sayings of Jesus Christ is: "The Kingdom of heaven is within you and whosoever knoweth himself shall find it. And having found it, ye shall know yourselves that ye are the sons and heirs of the Father, the Almighty, and shall know yourselves that ye are in God, and God in you. And ye are the City of God."[8]

Obviously, there are levels of self-knowledge and corresponding development or deepening of being. Different traditions refer to these levels in many ways: seven-storied mountain, rungs of a ladder, levels of consciousness. Within ourselves at the level of ordinary humanity, where we usually are, there is confusion and chaos. We are like "a troubled sea, a sea that cannot rest, whose troubled waters cast up mud and filth."[9] We have conflicting desires and compulsions in constant flux; there is nothing abiding, nothing that could properly be called *self*. As Pascal said, "We are naught but lies, duplicity, contradiction, and we hide and disguise ourselves from ourselves."[10] Only deeper down, is there the possibility of increased understanding, integration and wholeness. Only in a state of collectedness, composure, openness, and alertness can we know anything objectively. In all other states our perceiving apparatus is out of tune and introduces its own noise arising out of internal or external distractions and afflictions. Nothing that we decipher in these dispersed states is ultimately trustworthy. One of the purposes of the various spiritual schools is to help men repair themselves and gradually to come to a state of preparedness, freed of subjective desires, expectations, and fears. As long as we keep making our little noises, we cannot truly hear. Only when quietened within, may we encounter what is real.

In that purified, integrated state, arrived at after a long and arduous spiritual journey, we can discover our deepest self, which sages call by various names: "the spirit of the soul" (Eckhart), "*acumen mentis*" (Hugh of St Victor), "center of the soul" (St Teresa of Avila), "spark of the soul" (St Jerome), "the divine person who is beyond the beyond" (*Mundaka Upanishad*). These are all attempts to name the nameless, but as Eckhart said: "The God who is without a name is inexpressible, and the soul in its ground is equally inexpressible, as He is inexpressible . . . To gauge the soul we must gauge it with God, for the ground of God and the ground of soul are one and the same."[11] It is of this self of selves that the *Upanishads* speak when they declare: "Thou art that"; it is that Atman (Self) which is Brahman.[12] Only he who speaks from that center can say, "My Father and I are one . . . I am the way, the truth and the life; no one comes to the Father except by me."[13]

When we thus know ourselves, we no longer know *this* self or *that* self; we know the Self, unrestricted by any particularity. This knowledge is possible only when one's my-ness, one's ego is transcended. Strictly speaking, therefore, there is no one who is anyone who knows the Self; the Self knows itself. This is what Plotinus calls "a flight of the Alone to the Alone."[14] "Not I, the I that I am, know these things," says Boehme, "but God knows them in me." It is this Self into which we who labor and are heavy laden must go to find rest.[15] If abandoning all else, in this alone we take refuge, we shall be released from evil.[16]

In general, our consciousness is so thoroughly limited by space-time and language that we imagine all levels of being lie in these limits. Condemned to the surfaces as we are, we deny the depths altogether, forgetting that these limitations do not represent more than a tiny fragment of reality. Restricted consciousness, however, confines itself within these boundaries, into which it attempts to force everything else. It is as if the whole musical scale must be confined to a single note because that is all we can hear. Our ordinary language is an instrument for interpersonal transactions, not for suprapersonal ones. When one's ego is transcended, the word "I" loses meaning and significance; so does the subject-object dichotomy which depends on it. Once this linguistically central distinction becomes blurred, all description becomes problematic. Some then say, "I am *Brahman,*" and others that "The Father dwells in me," and some, like the Buddha, remain silent or give no positive description at all.

Giving up the ego is like the breaking of a large dam. The water gushes out with such force that it destroys

any nearby landforms. On the other hand, away from
the source the water flows in pre-existing channels.
As it becomes more distant from the source, unless
fed by some fresh springs, the water gets shallower
and dirtier and loses power to cleanse those who
bathe in it. Here the devouring outpouring of the
Spirit is channeled into the established forms of
languages, philosophies, and religions. Men lay claim
to these words, systems, and symbols, and quarrel over
them, in their egomania dragging the sacred down to
the profane.

THE ETERNAL TEACHING

Ultimately, a son of God brings no new teaching;
his teaching is *novel* but not *original*, for wisdom that
is eternal is not of time. It is the ancient way that he
uncovers and reveals afresh for a new generation. "I
have seen," the Buddha says, "the ancient way, the old
road that was taken by the formerly All-Awakened,
and that is the path I follow."[17] Yajnavalkya in the
oldest Upanishad quotes verses, already old by his
time, which mention "the narrow path which stretches
far away," by which "the wise are set free and
ascend."[18] This is why many people such as St
Augustine regard Christianity as older than the Jesus
of Nazareth; and why Gautama Buddha is sometimes
considered to be only one in a chain of previous
Buddhas. But nobody can arrogate to himself the
honor of being a high priest: he is called by God, as
was Christ in the succession of Melchizedek.[19]

What the master teaches is not *his*, for *he by himself*
is nobody.[20] His importance does not lie in the fact
that he is any particular one—from a specific place,
or lineage, or of a specific color, form, or shape.

Having become no one in particular, having sacrificed himself, he has been made worthy to open the scroll of hidden wisdom and to break its seven seals, so that he can behold that which no vision of ego can see. Having become nothing himself, he becomes the All. "I do not speak on my own authority, but the Father who sent me has himself commanded me what to say and how to speak."[21] The bridge to the other shore, the teaching, is not constructed from here to there. Any true path is laid only by the Spirit, from there to here. When the Buddha "roars his lion's roar," he continues, "now if anyone says of me, Gautama the Pilgrim, knows and sees as aforesaid, that my eminent Aryan gnosis and insight have no superhuman quality, and that I teach a Law that has been beaten out by reasoning, experimentally thought out and self-expressed, if he will not recant, not repent and abandon this view, he falls into hell."[22]

The teaching is superhuman; it is from above. It finds its expression in men specially chosen for their strength, understanding, and sacrifice, after they have been stripped bare, purified, and made whole. There are many vessels of different shapes and colors containing water from the same vast ocean. In general, most of them have been defiled by men like us—self-seeking and self-important. If we begin to make efforts to wake up, we may begin to see ourselves and beyond ourselves; we may then be able to distinguish between the genuine and the counterfeit. As long as we remain within the confines of our own little ego-shells, we are not twice born. We can, if we change our ways and work hard enough, give up the nothingness to which we cling and be born again, in the Spirit. We can attain the ocean of Buddhahood when the bottom of our little egoistic pail is broken.

Kabir sings:

> Water in the pail, pail in the water
> Water outside, water inside.
> Breaking the pail, water merges into water.
> This truth is all that the wise say.[23]

THE LIMITS OF REASON

One of the greatest obstacles on the spiritual path is said to be excessive argumentation and theorizing. "Make no mistake about this," says St Paul, "if there is anyone among you who fancies himself wise—wise, I mean, by the standards of the passing age—he must become a fool to gain true wisdom. For the wisdom of this world is folly in God's sight. Scripture says, 'He traps the wise in their own cunning,' and again, 'The Lord knows the arguments of the wise are futile.' "[24] Hardly any of the great spiritual teachers—Moses, Buddha, Mahavira, Jesus, Mohammed, Francis of Assisi, Ramakrishna—have been what we call a scholar or a learned man. Undoubtedly, they were *wise*; their wisdom is distinct from rational knowledge and is not acquired by book learning.

The reasoning faculty in man has this remarkable feature: it wishes to take control. And in order to be the master, it attempts to create an entire universe according to its own desires and purposes. This is true of all mental constructs, whether at the level of our personal lives or at the level of the general public enterprise of knowledge and manipulation of nature. The mind which is uneasy with what is, whittles away at it, ignores some parts and chooses others, until reality is forced into a framework which can be handled. Whatever does not fit into our conceptual schemes, even potentially, frightens us and we try to denigrate it by calling it "irrational," "irregular," or "secondary," while we glorify "reason" and "law"— all according to our ability and control. The mental universes that we create for our habitation are often at variance with each other, having been made according to our individual capacities, cravings, and imaginings. Occasionally, one of these constructs oversteps the commonly accepted bounds of fantasy, and we consider its maker insane. Nevertheless, all of us live in a fantastic world—abstracted and self-made— which keeps us shielded and veiled from truth. He who sees clearly is freed from this illusory world, this voluntary prison of the ego, and says with Aurobindo:

> I have escaped and the small self is dead;
> I am immortal, alone, ineffable;
> I have gone out from the universe I made,
>   And have grown nameless and immeasurable
> I am the one Being's sole immobile Bliss;
> No one I am, I who am all that is.[25]

Whatever be the nature of spiritual reality, it must engage and involve the whole human being and not only the discursive intellect. Ratiocination by itself, without checks of experience, leads to speculative extravagance and mere theorizing within the web of human reason alone. In this web are antinomies, dichotomies, and contradictions. Caught in it, man cannot get to the mystery and riddle of life. The history of philosophy is replete with intellectual giants struggling to build bridges between human reasoning and the yonder shore. Some of them—Plato, Plotinus, Augustine, Shankara, Thomas Aquinas, for example— finally take refuge in some sort of *intellectual contemplation* above and beyond ratiocination. Some others—Kant and Wittgenstein, to name only two—

deny that there is any link between rational knowledge and spiritual reality.

This is not to say that rational activity is necessarily
opposed to spiritual life. Reason, of course, has its
rightful and important place; however, it has the
tendency to usurp control by dominating feeling and
intuition.[26] It is not that our reason is overdeveloped
and needs to be curbed; our problem is that we are
merely rational and do not cultivate or listen to our
other faculties of perception. So we make one-sided
judgments, based only on reason, not in keeping with
the general harmony of our soul. In an integrated self,
the different inner parts function in their place, in
proper order, without contradicting each other. As
Plato describes it, just and beautiful action is that
which preserves and indeed helps to achieve this
inner harmony—between the reasonable, spirited,
and appetitive parts of our soul; wisdom is that knowledge which oversees this action.[27] As Pascal said, "Two
excesses: excluding reason, accepting reason only."

Exclusively theoretical speculation has always been
regarded as a distraction from the spiritual path. The
sage Yajnavalkya advised his wife not to question too
much lest her head fall off.[28] The major reason is
simply the insight, as with Kant, that reason cannot
escape its own antinomies and continues to wander
from question to question without any ultimate resolution. Regarding the path of the Buddha, we find:

> Should anyone say that he does not wish to lead
> the holy life under the Blessed One, unless the
> Blessed One first tells him whether the world is
> eternal or temporal, finite or infinite; whether the
> life principle is identical with the body, or some-
> thing different; whether the Perfect One continues
> after death, etc.—Such a one would die, ere the
> Perfect One could tell him all this.

It is as if a man were pierced by a poisoned arrow, and his friends, companions, or near relations called in a surgeon, but that man should say: "I will not have this arrow pulled out until I know who the man is that has wounded me: whether he is a noble, a prince, a citizen, or a servant"; or: "What his name is and to what family he belongs"; or: "whether he is tall or short or of medium height." Verily, such a man would die, ere he could adequately learn all this.[29]

The basic interest of a spiritual aspirant is not in a scientific-philosophical explanation of the world, but in seeing what his situation is and attempting to live in accordance with the requirements of his deeper self. Excessive speculations about how this world has come to be as it is are distracting and unhelpful, and do not lead to an inner change. The aspirant accepts the empirical situation as he finds it and searches for ways of deliverance from his slavery to inner and outer influences which keep him in bondage. He is not concerned with "knowledge" out of curiosity or for its own sake, as an end in itself.[30] His first and last concern is upward transformation which alone gives practical import to his search for liberation.

The Buddha remained silent in response to all metaphysical inquiries. "The *Tathagat* has no theories."[31] He insisted on the individual coming to an understanding of his own situation and following the way of his salvation. What the aspirant needs is a psycho-spiritual *path* for becoming, rather than a philosophical-metaphysical *system* of speculations and explanations. As long as we remain as we are, all thinking and talking about ideals, goals and ultimate reality is an escape from real work. In mountain climbing one seldom knows what the peak is like, but the last step depends on the first one; one must pay attention to it

if he does not want to fall. As one advances, he has a
better view of what was previously covered in mist. In
none of the traditional myths does the hero have a very
clear idea of what lies ahead. He cannot; we have a
picture of only the familiar and the known, not of the
mystery. This is as it should be, for we can understand
clearly only that which is below or at the level of our
understanding. "Had I a God whom I could understand," said Eckhart, "I would no longer hold him
for God."[32]

For a person more interested in experience than in
explanation, there is a very important methodological
reason for mistrusting speculative ideas. Ideas arise
in the world of definite names, shapes, and forms and
then acquire, as it were, an independent existence of
their own. Clusters of primitive ideas form more com-
plex and abstract ideas, which are then used by the
mind to interpret experience. Reality, or the given,
does not impinge on our minds directly; it does so
only through this network of ideas acquired by the
mind. Acquisition of these ideas, gathered by associa-
tion and analogy, is what we usually call *education*.
Often, the more "educated" a person is, the less open
he is to new experience; he perceives the world
through the thickened glasses of his ideas and according to their coloration. Spiritual teachers in all ages—
from the Upanishadic sages to Krishnamurti—have
urged a quieting of the mind, a suspension of *ideas*
regarding the nature of the soul or God or the world.
What they prescribe is an opening of oneself, in a state
of active passivity, and attending without tension to
what is. The "God" of philosophers—of Aristotle, of
Descartes, of Hegel—is most suspect. It is merely an
idea in somebody's head, needed to complete an intellectual system. It is this sort of god about whom one
has *arguments*, for or against, or whose existence is

subject to *proofs*. This mind-made God is yet another hurdle over which the aspirant has to jump. It is from this mental conjecture that Eckhart wants to be delivered when he says, "I ask God that he rid me of God."[33]

What we understand with our ideas is at least partly created by ourselves. We fashion the world in the mold of our ideas. Spiritual reality—whatever else it may be—is superhuman; it is not created or measured by human mind. It *reveals* itself to those who are prepared to receive it. All teachers have attempted to jog the minds of their students out of their accustomed grooves, so that something new is not immediately pigeonholed in familiar compartments. Some of the more dramatic methods which some Zen masters have used for this purpose are well known from the sensational spiritual press. However, shocks—administered appropriately by a master who himself is freed of his ego—have incalculable value in removing our usual idea props. One who is never lost cannot find himself. The danger of ideas is precisely in this: they tend to aid the mind in labelling new experiences with old names, classifying and systematizing, and thus gaining an impression that something has been understood. All that happens in the process is that the mind, after this classification, feels in control of the situation and gets comfortable again with its own old daydreaming and fantasizing. We go back to sleep—having heard the name perhaps, but not having seen the face.

KNOWLEDGE BY UNKNOWING

What is required is radical openness; with no *idea* of what we shall find, with no expectations, wishes, desires, or hopes. All of these are constraints on what is; they are prejudices. It is total emptying of oneself that is called for, complete nakedness, and a patient waiting for the "King of the dark chamber." What is asked is, indeed, sacrifice of the self; only then is the second birth.

> Now, if anyone should put the question, whether I admit any view at all, he should be answered thus: "The Perfect One (Buddha) is free from any theory, for the Perfect One has understood what the body is, and how it arises, and passes away. He has understood what mental formations are, and how they arise, and pass away. Therefore I say, the Perfect One has won complete deliverance through the extinction, fading away, disappearance, rejection, and getting rid of all opinions and conjectures, of all inclination to the vainglory of *I* and *mine*."[34]

What the aspirant searches and prepares himself for is something completely *objective*. It is transpersonal and universally verifiable, though not in the external manner of the modern natural sciences. It is not something private—fancied, imagined, desired. It is, in fact, not defiled, restricted, or contained by one's wishes, ideas, or thoughts. It is wrong even to say that one *seeks* ultimate reality, for one finds what one seeks—still within the web of one's own ideas and desires. "He who seeks God under settled form lays hold of the form, while missing the good concealed in it," said Eckhart.[35] In the long run, all striving and seeking—spiritual or otherwise—must stop. As a Buddhist scripture expresses it, "When the mind returns to its natural abode there is neither the path nor anyone who traverses it."[36] Nor is it finally quite possible to say that this reality is *objective*, for this label makes sense only from the point of view of a consciousness which is still divided. It is neither objective nor non-objective, nor a combination of the two. We can have no idea or description that can pin it down; there is nothing intelligible to our ordinary mind that can really be said of it. This is why it is "the Great Mystery," "the Abyss," "the Void," "the eternal Stillness."

This is how St John of the Cross puts it:

> I came into the unknown
> and stayed there unknowing,
> rising beyond all science.
>
> I was so far inside
> so dazed and far away
> my senses were released
> from feelings of my own.
> My mind had found a surer way:
> a knowledge by unknowing,
> rising beyond all science.
>
> This knowledge by unknowing
> is such a soaring force
> that scholars argue long
> but never leave the ground.
> Their knowledge always fails the
> source:
> to understand unknowing,
> rising beyond all science.[37]

"OBJECTIVE" KNOWLEDGE

When we think of *objectivity*, we immediately think of science. However, the objectivity of the natural sciences is not so radical nor really complete. Scientific activity is much more aggressive; it is an assertion of the human ego. Man poses questions to nature and tortures her to yield answers. The experiments and observations he makes cannot be independent of his own theories and conjectures.[38] It is not possible to make a scientific observation without a prior theoretical system. In science, any theory is better than no theory. In order to get going, scientists have been (and are) happy to have partial, incomplete, or wrong theories rather than wait for a correct one; until a new theory is available, the old one is not abandoned.[39] This was clearly recognized by Newton, the giant of the scientific revolution which heralded modern science. It is not far off the mark to say that modern science took off at the point when scientists shifted their allegiance from *truth* to *theorizing*, from internal *experience* to external *experiment*. Immanuel Kant made some very perceptive remarks concerning this:

> Reason, holding in one hand its principles, according to which concordant phenomena alone can be admitted as laws of nature, and in the other hand the experiment, which it has devised according to those principles, must approach nature, in order to be taught by it: but not in the character of a pupil, who agrees to everything the master likes, but as *an appointed judge, who compels the witnesses to answer the questions which he himself proposes.*[40]
> (Italics added)

The sciences are not really objective, for they never let the object reveal itself, as it is.[41] Objectivity is possible only if the object is reflected, whole and rich, in the clear pool of consciousness without the disturbing undulations of subjectivity—ideas, hopes, fears. Such an objectivity has its existence and meaning precisely in that undisturbed relationship and not in any description or knowledge apart from it. Since the scientists are concerned about producing public knowledge, and not about stilling their subjective agitations while relating to an object, they cannot be

objective in this sense. What is called *objectivity* in
the sciences is in fact *inter-subjectivity*. What is important is to find a description of an object about
which members of the scientific community—who
are members because they have come to share certain
basic assumptions and procedures—would agree with
each other.

This inter-subjective agreement is achieved by
several fundamental and far-reaching assumptions.[42]
In the first place, reality is considered to present itself
to nuclear individuals so that the object and the subject are inalienably distinct and separable from each
other. We have the testimony of many mystics and
artists that in their deeper experiences the subject-
object distinction is not as sharp as it usually appears
to our ordinary consciousness. Secondly, underlying
the experienced reality is posited an abstract and
purely rational construct; this construct is then
labeled "reality" and the experienced reality is labeled
"appearance." The scientific pursuit, then, is to
speculate about "reality" and to put these speculations
to the test, not of all "appearance," but only of those
parts which have a connection with the conjectured
"reality." Thus, both scientific theorizing and ex-
perimentation contain large elements of projection,
selection, and interpretation by reason. Thirdly, the
human being is considered essentially a rational
cognizer; his other faculties of perception are almost
wholly ignored. In the process, those aspects of reality
which correspond to our sensations and feelings—
such as color, smell, taste, beauty, purpose—are either
completely set aside or are denigrated to a secondary
status. For example, we know the charge and the mass
of an electron, but it is considered ludicrous to ask
what its color is and what it smells like.

The knowledge acquired by the imposition of this

metaphysical straightjacket on reality is like the confession obtained, under coercion, from an adversary. Anyone who objects to such procedures is suspected by the contemporary intellectual orthodoxy of succumbing to hopeless romanticism or irrational mysticism—opposed to reason and progress.

The "nature" that comes through the natural sciences is not as she is, but only that construction which the human reason has imposed upon her. Neils Bohr, a prominent scientist of the twentieth century, recognized this clearly: "It is wrong to think that the task of physics is to find out how nature is. Physics concerns what we can say about nature."[43] Even this description is further limited only to that which can be measured and quantified. From the scientific point of view, "that which cannot be measured is not real," as Max Planck said. The general tendency in the sciences is to reduce everything to a mechanistic level at which we get mathematical description of matter in motion, without meaning and purpose. The metaphysical underpinnings of the scientific procedure may be suitable for the investigation of inanimate reality. However, to attempt to copy the same methodology for understanding every order of being—higher as well as lower—is to tacitly assume the supremacy of the material over the spiritual. Inevitably, for us science-nurtured moderns, *cosmology* has become, as a matter of course, a branch of *physics*.

Thus we impoverish the universe in order to investigate it exclusively from *our* point of view, which cannot be any other than of control and manipulation. By an extension of our egocentricity, we believe that ordinary man, as he is, is the measure of all things.[44] By such a belief, we set ourselves over and against nature; we even speak of man in the universe as though we were not a part of it. This underlying attitude is common to all the contemporary sciences, arts, and humanities. Surely, this is at the root of our modern crisis. But, even when we recognize the crisis and genuinely wish to do something about it, we generally think of further technological manipulations in nature in the service of man. Our inner selves feel quite estranged from this abstracted world concocted by our possessive and aggressive reason, for there is no place for anything higher in it. We cannot find our own bearings in this vast cosmos because we imagine that everything in it has its place only with respect to us.

KNOWLEDGE OF HIGHER TRUTH

What is needed is a radical shift in our point of view. It is possible that the whole universe is not organized for our sake; perhaps it has its own purposes. Consider, for example, the fact that on the average one hundred million people die every year. One hundred million people—just like you and me—with their consciousnesses, their hopes and fears, their struggles and pleasures, with their dreams for their children and grandchildren. Of course, a hundred million or more are also born every year: new souls with fresh aspirations and hopes. It is hard to escape the image of the planet Earth as a huge creature with an extremely fecund womb and very destructive jaws, turning to its own rhythms and purposes, quite unmindful of the self-importance of any human being. Maybe all cosmic constellations—the earth, the Sun and the galaxies—have their functions and purposes. How can we find out what these may be; how can we hear and see? Surely, we can understand our place and purpose only from a point which is beyond ourselves, and to which we pay heed. As a *Upanishad* says, "Meditation (*dhyana*) assuredly, is more than thought. The earth meditates, as it were. The waters meditate . . . . The mountains meditate . . . . Gods and men meditate . . . . Therefore, whoever among men here attains greatness, he has obtained it, as it were as a share of the reward of meditation."[45] In meditation alone, in a state of active receptivity, can we hear the whispers from the other shore bringing clarity about our work on this shore, and about the higher and larger purposes which we are required to serve—either willingly and mindfully, or unwillingly and mindlessly.

Whatever we can study from *our* point of view—whether it is universe, man, or God—has been produced at least partly according to *our* plans; it is something that can be *compelled by us* to yield answers to *our* questions. It cannot be higher than us. That which is higher cannot be coerced or violated by us. We can prepare ourselves for it and wait, actively making an effort without violence, for what may be granted. "No one knows the Father but the Son and those to whom the Son may choose to reveal Him."[46]

It appears from the literature that momentary flashes of insight can occur to those who are not at all prepared to receive them. They can also be seized by violent means, such as the use of certain drugs and some practices involving breathing exercises. All spiritual authorities have warned against such means, for violence against the Spirit is the very essence of evil. It is very doubtful that the experiences gained have any real value, unless accompanied by a change in attitude away from self-gratification. It is only our mania for excitement and shortcuts that makes us assume that such peak experiences as the mystical ecstacies are the essence and aim of Self-realization, and then to insist that these experiences are similar to those induced by drugs.

That which is of the Spirit can be known only by making room for it to grow and manifest itself. No amount of speculation, argumentation, or aggression can help us appropriate the Spirit; what we can do is to prepare ourselves so that we may be appropriated by the Spirit. "To find or know God in reality by any outward proofs, or by anything but God himself made manifest and self-evident in you," writes the English mystic William Law, "will never be your case either here or hereafter. For neither God, nor heaven, nor hell, nor the devil, nor the flesh, can be any otherwise knowable in you or by you, but by their own existence and manifestation in you. And all pretended knowledge of any of these things, beyond and without this self-evident sensibility of their birth within you is only such knowledge of them as the blind man hath of the light that hath never entered into him."[47]

The movement from oneself to the Self is an ascent along the hierarchy of being and consciousness. Only this becoming constitutes genuine knowledge of the divine. Theology cannot be merely a rational, scientific inquiry; it is transformation first and last. An inner growth, a development towards divinity, is essential if we would approach the truths which are at higher levels. As a Hindu scripture has it, "no one who is not himself divine can successfully worship divinity."[48] Jesus Christ said, "And no man hath ascended up to heaven, but he that came down from heaven, even the son of man which is in heaven."[49]

PREPARATION

In any kind of learning the amount of truth accessible to a student depends on the training and preparation he has had. If a non-physicist were to come across an equation like $G_{uv} = 8\pi T_{uv}$ he can make no sense of it. If he is told that these are the famous field equations in Einstein's Theory of General Relativity, relating space-time curvature with distribution of mass-energy density, he may be amused, intrigued, or annoyed, but he cannot understand it with his ordinary notions of time, curvature, or energy. A long scientific training and background is required to comprehend fully the meaning, importance, and limitations of these equations.[50] Presumably, the supreme identities like "Atman is Brahman" and "My Father and I are one" are not easy to comprehend without right preparation. Every spiritual tradition emphasizes a long and hard training in order to understand its great formulations. Unlike scientific or philosophic understanding, however, spiritual understanding is not only intellectual and external; it is not complete unless the aspirant verifies these formulations in his own experience, in the core of his being.

In spiritual knowing, the student himself is both the subject and the object, as well as the place where this knowledge takes place. The preparation required here is the sharpening and honing of his instrument, of the person himself. The spiritual training is not only of a part of oneself but of the whole person—body, mind and soul. Only when our separate parts have been brought to some integration can we pay attention and wait upon what is higher. As a *Upanishad* says,

> Not he who has not desisted from evil ways, not he who is not tranquil, not he who has not a concentrated mind, not even he whose mind is not composed can reach this *Atman* through right knowledge.[51]

The spiritual evolution calls for giving up of our self-importance and other cherished illusions which hinder our seeing reality. "Liberation is accomplished by wisdom," says Shankara, "but wisdom does not arise without the purification of the heart." Many teachers have indicated some habits and properties which strengthen our bonds of ignorance, which keep us knotted and afflicted. These are sins in the sense that "to sin is to do an injury to yourself."[52] The emphasis put on any one or more of these has varied according to the needs of their disciples. These include the seven deadly sins of Christianity—pride, envy, anger, dejection, avarice, gluttony, and lust.[53] In the *Bhagavad Gita* all of these are mentioned among "demoniacal properties conducive to bondage," but three in particular—lust, anger and greed—are declared to "constitute the triple gate to hell."[54] Ramakrishna repeatedly warned his disciples against lust and greed as being the two major obstacles to spiritual development. Gurdjieff regarded vanity and self-love as the two chief agents of the devil.

Siddhartha, the future Buddha, while engaged in spiritual efforts was approached and tempted to abandon the great struggle by *Mara*, the Evil One, accompanied by his hosts, namely lust, discontent, hunger and thirst, craving, sloth and laziness, cowardice, doubt, hypocrisy and stupidity, gain, fame, honor and glory falsely obtained, exaltation of self, and contempt of others. There are several other legends concerning temptation and threats by *Mara* to deviate the Buddha from his path, including universal sovereignty, bodily harm and death, desire to transmute the *Himalaya* mountain into gold.[55] Similar temptations were faced by Jesus when he was led by the Spirit up and down the wilderness for forty days.[56]

With so many pitfalls and temptations, it is no wonder that the spiritual path is always considered

very difficult. The *Katha Upanishad* (1.3:14) declares
the path "sharp as a razor's edge." the *Dhammapada*
(6:85) tells us that "few are there among men who
arrive on the other shore."[57] "Enter by the narrow
gate. The gate is wide that leads to perdition, there is
plenty of room on the road, and many go that way: but
the gate that leads to life is small and the road is
narrow, and those who find it are few."[58] Jesus himself
at Gethsemane wondered if he could endure the final
sacrifice. "My Father, if it is possible, let this cup
pass me by. Yet not as I will, but as thou wilt."[59]

Just as there are qualities conducive to bondage,
there are others helpful in liberation. It is not to be
understood, however, that there are sins to be overcome and virtues to be acquired and then, auto-
matically, one is free. Various virtues mark a free man;
they are his characteristics. That is how we recognize
a liberated man, just as we know a person to be
demoniacal if he possesses qualities like hypocrisy,
arrogance, pride, anger, harshness, and ignorance.
Similarly, one who is naturally endowed with divine
virtues is fearless, pure in heart, steadfast in the exercise of wisdom, generous, and self-controlled, ascetic,
upright, non-violent, truthful, free from anger, at
peace, averse to calumny, free from nagging greed,
gentle, modest, ardent, patient, enduring, pure, free
from malice and pride.[60]

RADICAL TRANSFORMATION

The fact that ethical effort is necessary in one's
spiritual development does not mean that what one
seeks and prepares oneself for is an ethical state. Along
with conceptual and other dichotomies, the ethical
opposition of good and evil is also transcended by the
liberated sage. "He is not affected by good or evil for

then he has passed beyond all the sorrows of the heart," says a *Upanishad.*[61] As Eckhart said, "there neither vice nor virtue ever entered in."[62] Or, as another *Upanishad* has it: It is we who may interpret the sage's actions as "good," and his behavior as giving some meaning to our notions of "virtue." He is not circumscribed by our standards for he is freed from them. Our laws do not govern him. Unlike us, he acts spontaneously from his own inner nature, having ended the law.

So long as we act from the ego, every "virtuous act" turns sour. Anything at all—good works, charity, service to others, scholarship, meditation—can be pressed into the service of the ego; these activities can be guided by appearance, pride, vanity, jealousy, fear, or greed. The rewards we hanker after can be in this world or in the world beyond, according to our imaginings. Although all of the spiritual teachers have advised doing good work and service to others, they have repeatedly emphasized that it is the inner reorientation which is primary; we must first seek the kingdom of God, which alone makes it possible for us to see what needs to be done and how. An aspirant labors and toils not in order to change the world first, but in order to transform himself; so long as he remains as he is, he cannot bring about any essential change in anything. A man should first be purged of all egotism before he is qualified to help the world. It is easier to presume to help others than to realize that one needs help oneself. When one is driven by craving for name and fame, wealth and power, approval and acceptance, or for gaining of heaven and salvation, one does not know how to help others; most of the utopian dreams and revolutions are disappointing. The primary revolution is a revolution in oneself. Krishnamurti has said it well:

Change within the pattern is no change at all; it is mere modification, reformation. Only by breaking away from the social pattern without building another can you 'help' society. As long as you belong to society, you are only helping it to deteriorate. All societies, including the most marvelously utopian, have within them the seeds of their own corruption. To change society, you must break away from it. You cease to be what society is: acquisitive, ambitious, envious, power-seeking, and so on.[63]

By struggling with our own lower nature we can begin to recognize our situation and discover what keeps our vision clouded. It is as if we needed to open another door of perception in order to have glimpses of reality which we cannot see as we are. We have to discover and look with our third eye, for the two physical ones see only dimly. It is only this third which can see the hidden sun, for "to any vision must be brought an eye adapted to what is to be seen, and having some likeness to it. Never did eye see the sun unless it had first become sun-like, and never can the soul have vision of the First Beauty unless itself be beautiful."[64]

The effort required to awaken is particularly hard in the beginning, as is also true in rousing from ordinary sleep. All the soporific forces of stupor and ignorance seem to redouble their activities at the very first step towards uncovering the small amount of pure gold necessary for more gold to be obtained from baser metals. This was clearly seen by some of the alchemists in their metallurgical allegory for the transformation of man. Only "he who has will be given more," for "light is visible by light."[65] The little flame of conscience and search that we have needs to be protected and nurtured; this alone could help us kindle the fire of effort and suffering in which our pretensions and vanities may be transmuted.

What is needed is a transformation of our being which is completely radical, that is to say, from the very roots. No social or psychological adjustment would do. It is a sign of confusion and misunderstanding to assume that the aim of the spiritual paths such as Yoga, Zen, Sufism is the same as that of modern schools of psychotherapy. This is not to say that the former do not have much of therapeutic value. Mental health may accrue from Yoga, but that is not its aim; if anything, mental health is a prerequisite to a serious study of Yoga. All psychotherapeutic schools are concerned with the proper and self-fulfilling functioning of a person within a socio-cultural framework, whereas the spiritual schools aim at total reorientation and yoking of the whole individual to a transcendent purpose, that is, a purpose other than his own.[66] *Spiritual* refers only to that which pertains to the Spirit, above and beyond any personal consciousness, psyche, ego or soul.

The healing which is involved in the spiritual paths is that of wholeness and holiness. It is not someone's personal neurosis or personality defect that Yoga wishes to cure; it is the whole human condition that is of interest; the *malady*, if one may so speak, arises from the very fact of being human. As St Paul said, "we wrestle not against flesh and blood, but against principalities, powers, rulers of the darkness of this world, and spiritual wickedness in high places."[67]

RECONCILING OPPOSITES

However, one does not struggle against these large forces single-handedly, or only with one's own power. The upward force also is more than personal. Man is between these two large forces; he comes into existence owing to their interplay and is always subject to them. Man's life is like the river connecting the two shores of his being; both are needed for a man's existence to have a definite form. The *Bhagavad Gita* speaks of two major tendencies—godly and demonic, or upward and downward. Both make demands and create compulsions. Given the thoroughly value-laden, hierarchic system of all spiritual teachings, we should recognize one demand as *calling* and the other as *temptation*. Man is between these two currents; his only choice seems to be to align himself either with the one or with the other, remembering, of course, as Jesus Christ said, that "he that is not with me is against me; and he that gathereth not with me scattereth abroad."[68]

Among the subtlest temptations along any spiritual path are the psychic powers which often seem to accompany practice. Without the appropriate inner or outer guidance, the possibility of egotistic manipulation of these powers is immense. Such personal use of these powers is the essence of black magic, and one needs to be constantly on guard against such misappropriation. Psychic powers, just like the athletic ones, belong to the material nature in man; except that they belong to a subtler part of nature. All great spiritual authorities have warned against excessive fascination with these powers. This fascination can divert one from the true path leading to the Source, by involvement in interesting side effects. Increase in power without the corresponding development of wisdom and humility is bound to lead to ruination.

History seems to suggest the operation of definite laws by which the sacred impulses given by the great spiritual teachers can change direction and even reverse themselves completely. A corruption of the teachings appears inevitable unless, by the conscious efforts of the followers, the original impulses are kept from deflection or dissipation. Whenever we take a teaching in a partial manner, as we do when we see merely analytically or sentimentally, we distort it and prepare the way for its degeneration. Thus, we turn recognition of one's nothingness-as-one-is into dejection and fatalism; the idea of the state of consciousness beyond good and evil into a metaphysics of licentiousness; self-surrender into self-mortification; the state beyond logic into irrationality; search for Self into self-seeking of personal salvation; transcendence of worldliness into flight from the world; detachment from the fruits of actions into inaction. All these arise because we reason in terms of dualities in a single dimension. Thus we set up rigid oppositions between the flesh and the Spirit, maya and Brahman, samsara and nirvana, world and God, self and Self, as if they were both at the same level and one of them must be eliminated in order to acknowledge the other.

Rather than exclusion of the one or the other, what is called for is recentering of ourselves. Our efforts and search for the Self are in and through the self. *Sacred* and *profane* are not ontological categories; they are psychological attitudes. "One's own mind, indeed, is *samsara* (world); let a man cleanse it by effort."[69] There is nothing that is unholy and inalienably in conflict with the holy. There are only sacred and profane points of view: one is spiritual, comprehensive, and integrative; the other is egoistic, partial, and exclusivist. And the two are engaged in a battle in, and for, our own soul. We can let ourselves be pulled down to the level of animality in us, or we can make efforts to open ourselves to be transformed into a higher being. One who is centered in the Spirit does not cease living and working in the world; in him such contradictions are resolved. Born of the Spirit, he becomes like Christ, the Man-God, in whom "the world is reconciled to God."[70] Then, as indeed now, nirvana and samsara are one. For a person spiritualized and made whole, true enjoyment of the world can begin, and he can be a priest at "the marriage of heaven and hell" (Blake), for "whoever is born of God doth not commit sin."[71]

SPIRITUAL BECOMING

We, however, who are on this side of the veil, are not reconciled within ourselves. For us neither the journey nor the law has ended. And no amount of verbal trickery can get us off the hook of contradiction on which we squirm and flail—slowly dying. Religions, philosophies, sciences, and psychologies, as they are available in the present age, do not seem to address themselves to the practical details of movement to another point, along the vertical axis of being, from which alone another vision can become possible. When they speak to such issues at all, what they offer are comfort or resignation, "peak experiences" or amnesia, and, above all, mazes of words and facts. In the so-called explosion of knowledge, there are words about facts, facts and words, often signifying little of true worth. So long as it does not help us wake up, all learned talk is what Gurdjieff has called "pouring-from-the-empty-into-the-void."[72]

If we are primarily interested in being rather than talking, in experience rather than explanation, in knowing who we are rather than in winning positions, arguments, and converts, what we need is a path of spiritual becoming rather than a system of theological talking. How can we be learnedly voluble about the question of the identity of Atman and Brahman when we have no experience of either one or the other? Does something vital depend on our belief or disbelief in the doctrine of the trinity? Is our problem really that we do not know what the Christ or the Buddha actually said? What would we do when the next month's scholarly journals bring out the erudite dissertations of professors of theology on God or nirvana or maya? Perhaps God is alive this year or perhaps dead; transcendent or immanent; revolutionary or evolutionary; perhaps female or black; perhaps Hindu or Christian or ecumenical; we still suffer—with occasional glimpses of the trap we are in, not knowing why we are in it and how to escape. The trap is of non-being and non-awareness; the way out must teach us how to be and how to know.

The way must begin from where we are, not from an ideal somewhere else. The ideal may give meaning and direction to the way by its presence and challenge; but we who suffer over the gulf separating us from the ideal have to learn to approach it. As we are, the peak of the mountain of being cannot be very clear to us; all we can have are theories, ideas, and imaginings. An occasional clearing of the mist reveals the lower slopes and our reason is baffled. Unless we are watchful and on guard, our possessive mind begins to philosophize in order to capture and fashion the unknown along its own ideas. Bewildered, we scramble for the security of some theory, doctrine, or argument which we can appropriate. Unless we are engaged in the practical struggle of re-orienting ourselves—body, mind and soul—to what is higher, nirvana and God, within or above, remain only crutches for security, although we can speak about them with much erudition or sentiment. "The kingdom of God is not a matter of talk, but of power," says St Paul.[73] We have the advice of all spiritual traditions to leave vain

speculations and theories aside and to learn to walk
along the edge of the blade of life—neither denying
nor affirming, neither believing nor doubting, but
trying to be present to the experience of ourselves
and whatever is.

In our searchings—whether we are from the East
or the West—we grope in the same area of darkness:
ignorance of our selves and of our place and of purpose
in the cosmos. When our questions are serious, they
cannot have the kind of answers which can be provided by books, systems, or religions. When we are
quiet and listening to ourselves, we know that we have
no choice: we must try to respond to these questions;
they contain all our essential possibilities. Traditions
and teachers can sustain us and point the way to
another mode of existence; but it is we who must
tread the path; it is our cross and our opportunity.

We must begin not from metaphysics but from experience, recognizing ourselves as we are: disinte-
grated, confused and without will, "like chaff driven
by the wind."[74] We do not want to keep in sight the
horror of our situation, and we continue imagining we
are somebody important and building fantastic
theories about our free will, our immortal souls, and
the life beyond. From our very birth, we are subjected
to this mass psychosis, this refusal to face up to the
human condition, by engaging in frenzied activity,
accumulating information, possessions, and pleasures.
Thoroughly self-willed and self-centered, we are bent
on self-expression and self-fulfillment; yet we are
afraid to know ourselves. When we look at ourselves
without self-pity and self-justification, we find ourselves knotted up and conflicted, doing things which
we do not want to do, and saying what we do not want
to say. "I do not even acknowledge my own actions as
mine, for what I do is not what I want to do, but what I

detest," says St Paul. "The good which I want to do, I fail to do; but what I do is the wrong which is against my will."[75] Similarly, Arjuna asks in the *Bhagavad Gita*, "Krishna, what is it that makes a man do evil, even against his own will; under compulsion, as it were?"[76]

A recognition of the compulsions under which we live, of our afflictions and suffering, our sinful condition, our lower nature, is the first rent in the shroud of illusions by which we cover ourselves. In the isolation of our self-exile, we fancy ourselves as the king of the castle, which we struggle hard to protect. If we see ourselves flailing in our worldly agitation, completely under the sway of forces over which we have no control, we can begin to understand and accept the fact of our nothingness. When our soul sees its true face in the mirror of the Spirit, it knows what needs to be done. Guided by our conscience and helped by higher influences, we can allow a transformation of ourselves, and become "fused and not confused" (Eckhart).

When a man begins to wake up, he is no longer at peace with himself. Peace is for those who are either sound asleep or are fully awake. In between is the struggle: a step forward, a relapse, a fall, another moment of seeing—the unknown playing hide-and-seek with the known. In this rite of life, my little ego is the sacrificial animal. My bruised self wants me to run away and take shelter. But remorse of the dimly recognized conscience keeps gnawing at me for my cowardice, blindness, and lies. The One who calls stares mercilessly at my holding back and clinging to my emptiness and suffering.

From across the river the sound of the flute calls and demands:

"What do you seek?"
"What do you serve?"
"How?"

Notes and References

Biblical quotations are from the King James Bible and the New English Bible.

CHAPTER 1

1. In P. D. Ouspensky, *In Search of the Miraculous—Fragments of an Unknown Teaching* (London: Routledge, Kegan Paul Ltd., 1957), p. 219.
2. *The Gospel of Shri Ramakrishna*, Trans. with an introduction by Swami Nikhilananda (Madras: Mylapore, 1947), p. 170.
3. Psalms 82:6; II Peter 1:4; I John 3:1-2. Also St. Athanasius, "He became man that we might be made God" (*Athan. Orat. de Incarn Verbi. Tom.* 1, p. 108).
4. Matthew 16:24.
5. T. S. Eliot in "East Coker" in *Four Quartets* (London: Faber and Faber, 1966), p. 32.
6. *Theologia Germanica*, chapter 34.
7. John 18:36.
8. James 4:4 and I John 2:15.
9. John 17:15.
10. Matthew 16:26.
11. John 3:7-8.
12. *Maitri Upanishad* 3:2.
13. *Bhagavad Gita* 16:13-15.
14. John 8:28; 8:50; 14:10.
15. See René Guénon, *The Crisis of the Modern World*, trans. by A. Osborne (London: Luzac & Co., 1942), chapter V, for a discussion of this point.
16. Martin Buber, *Ten Rungs: Hasidic Sayings* (New York: Schocken Press, 1947), p. 103. This egoistic "I am" is entirely different from the "I AM" of the fullness of being uttered, for

117

example, in Exodus 3:14 or by Christ at many places in John.

17. *Buddhi*, which constitutes the subtlest and the highest faculty in man, is not translated easily. In translating the parable of the chariot in the *Katha Upanishad* (1.3:3-4), Radhakrishnan (*The Principal Upanishads*; New York: Harper & Brothers, 1953, p. 623) renders it as *intellect*; Aurobindo (*Eight Upanishads*; Pondicherry: Sri Aurobindo Ashram, 1965, p. 49) as *Reason*, Zimmer (*Philosophies of India*; New York: World Publ. Co., 1961, p. 363) by *intuitive discernment and awareness*, Zaehner (The *Bhagavad-Gita*; Oxford University Press, 1969, p. 238) by *soul*. (Zaehner's authority for this translation is based on the passage 2:41 of the *Gita* in which it is declared that the essence of the *buddhi* is will, which in the Christian tradition inheres in the "soul.") In other connections, these authors and others employ other words to translate *buddhi*. Some of these are: wisdom, consciousness, awareness. The verbal root *budh* means "to wake up; to rise from sleep; to heed, attend to; to perceive, to notice, learn, understand, become aware of; to have insight into, understand thoroughly." *Buddhi* then means, returning to consciousness; presence of mind, intentions, purpose, design; perception, comprehension; intellect, understanding, intelligence, talent; discrimination, judgment, and discernment. In the *Sankhya-Karika* (23) *buddhi* is defined as *adhyayasaya*, i.e., "determination, resolution, mental effort; cognition, awareness."

Buddhi is above *manas* (mind, thinking faculty, ratiocination) and comprises the totality of man's emotional and intellectual possibilities. This is why it is termed *mahan* (the Great One). It is also known as *Prajna* (wisdom, discernment), *dhi* (intuition, imagination), *Khyati* (knowledge, power of distinguishing objects by appropriate names), *smrti* (memory, remembrance), *chitta* (comprising both functions of the reasoning faculty and the heart, viz., observing, thinking, desiring, and intending.) It is integrated intelligence.

It is useful to retain the Sanskrit word *buddhi* because any rendering into English is problematic. In my judgment, the closest one-word translation is *soul* as distinct from *mind* as well as *Spirit* or *Self*. If one used the tripartite division of *psyche* made by Plotinus, integrated or purified *buddhi* is the highest element which is directed to the contemplation of the *Nous* and the One; before purification, buddhi corresponds approximately to the middle element which may be attracted upwards or downwards. For a discussion of the importance of buddhi and buddhi yoga in the *Bhagavad Gita* and its parallels in Greek thought, see A. H.

Armstrong and R. Ravindra, "The Dimensions of the Self: *Buddhi* in the *Bhagavad Gita* and *psyche* in Plotinus," *Religious Studies*, vol. 15, 1979.
18. Isaiah 6:69.
19. Galatians 2:20.
20. This duality is not necessarily ultimately (ontologically) real. In some traditions, such as the *Advaita Vedanta* of Shankara, such dualism is vigorously opposed. However, the conflict of our higher and lower selves is a matter of experience, and can in practice be resolved only when the lower finds its place in a higher synthesis, which is not achieved by ratiocination alone.
21. Colossians 1:21.
22. The Greek word *metanoia*, usually rendered as *repentance* in the standard translations of the New Testament, is literally *change of mind*. See A. K. Coomaraswamy, "On being in One's Right Mind," *Review of Religion*, New York, VII, 1942, pp. 32-40, for some discussion.
23. Jacob Boehme, *A Dialogue between a Scholar and his Master concerning the Supersensual Life:* Dialogue II.
24. I Corinthians 2:16; 3:19.
25. Ephesians 4:22-24; 5:14.
26. Galatians 6:14.
27. There is a similar doctrine in St Thomas Aquinas (*Sum. Theol.* 1.34.1 and 2). Clearly, the *superconscious no-mindness* being referred to here is not to be confused with the *subconscious mindlessness* of lower humanity.
28. Plotinus, *Enneads* vi. 9.10.
29. *Gottam Sn.* 455-6. Compare with the incident described in Matthew (12:46-50) when Christ did not recognize his mother and brothers. The Buddha said, "I am not anyone anywhere, nor is there anywhere aught of mine" (*Anguttara Nikaya* 2:177).
30. Hebrews 7:3.
31. Parmenides, *Diels, Fr.* 185; Plotinus, *Enneads* vi. 9.
32. T. S. Eliot, "The Dry Salvages" in *Four Quartets, op. cit.*
33. Meister Eckhart: Sermon: Adolescens, tibi dico: surge!
34. Ludwig Wittgenstein, *Tractatus Logico Philosophicus*, Proposition 6.4311. Meister Eckhart says of eternity: "Everything stands in a present now."
35. "The Self's Infinity" in Sri Aurobindo, *Last Poems* (Pondicherry: Sri Aurobindo Ashram, 1952).
36. *Brihadaranyaka Upanishad* II, 4:14.
37. Deuteronomy 4:24.
38. Ephesians 4:13.

CHAPTER 2

1. Matthew 23:2-30. (*The Holy Bible*, Revised Standard Version, (New York: Thomas Nelson & Sons).
2. John 3:3.
3. *Majjhima Nikaya, Sutta* 63.
4. Erich Fromm, *You Shall Be as Gods* (London: Johnathan Cape, 1966), p. 227.
5. I John 2:9-11; 4:18-20; Matthew 7:21.
6. In the original, the lines are very simple and beautiful and employ a charming play on the word *manaka*, which means both *head* and *of the heart* (*mind*). In the original, the lines are:
> Manaka pherat yug bhaya,
> Bhaya na manaka phera.
> Karaka manaka chandike,
> Manaka manaka phera.
7. Matthew 7:29, John 3:11.
8. *One Hundred Poems of Kabir*, Trans. by Rabindranath Tagore, assisted by Evelyn Underhill (London: Macmillan & Co., 1967), no. XLII.
9. *Maitri Upanishad* 2:1, and John 3:8.
10. C. G. Jung, "Psychological Commentary on 'The Tibetan Book of the Great Liberation,'" in his *Psychology and Religion— West and East*, Bollingen Series XX (1958), p. 482.
11. Swami Sardananda, *Shri Shri Ramakrishna Lilāprasang* (Calcutta: Udobodhan Office, 1955), pp. 319-20.
12. William Blake, *The Everlasting Gospel*, a.

CHAPTER 3

1. Swami Prabhavananda, *The Spiritual Heritage of India* (New York: Doubleday, 1963), p. 67
2. *Mandukya Upanishad* 7.
3. *Mandukya Upanishad* 2, *Chandogya Upanishad* 6:9ff.
4. S. N. Dasgupta, *Hindu Mysticism* (New York: Freidrich Ungar Publ., 1959), p. 3.
5. *Rig Veda* ii, 6.5.
6. Dasgupta, *op. cit*, pp. 3-30.
7. The goddess *Vak* (Speech) occupies a very important place in the *Vedas*. Vak could be looked upon as accompanying and supporting all the gods, and reaching wherever the magic power of *Brahman* extends. The idea bears resemblance to the *Word of God* as personified in the Wisdom of Solomon and the logos of Philo, but it did not lead to the same development in cosmogenic

doctrine. Vak appears in the *Rig Veda* as an active female divine power showing grace to mortals. In the later Brahmanic period, Vak becomes more and more like the Greek *Logos*.

8. These events are *supernatural* only in the sense of being *supernormal*, that is, uncommon, unusual and extraordinary. St Augustine makes a useful distinction when he says that we must not regard wonders and signs as "contrary to nature," but only "contrary to what is known of nature" (*de Civ. Dei, Bk.* xxi, ch. viii).

9. Dasgupta, *op. cit.*, pp. 9-18.

10. According to the Indian notions of time and transmigration, in fact every being—human, god, or demon—is *immortal* in the sense that his existence continues endlessly in time, subject to successive births and deaths, forever. Therefore, what a spiritual aspirant seeks is beyond mere immortality; he aims at an existence in a timeless realm where there is no birth nor death. In the *Harinyakashipa* story, however, the word *immortal* means *continued existence in the same body.*

11. *Brihadaranyaka Upanishad* I.1.1-2.

12. *Atharva Veda* 12.3.13.

13. Both immortality and death are his shadows and not his substance, he being in reality above and beyond both.

14. *Rig Veda* X.129, 6-7.

15. *Katha Upanishad* 11.1:5, 10.

16. *Mundaka Upanishad* 3.2:9.

17. *Katha Upanishad* I.2:23; I.2:7-9; I.3:14.

18. The *Upanishads* are also a part of the *Vedas* which are generally divided into four parts: the *Samhitas* (hymns), the *Brahmans* (ritual texts), the *Aranyaks* (forest treatises), and the *Upanishads* (philosophical discourses).

19. The *Vedanta Sutras* are also known as *Brahma Sutras* because they expound the philosophy of *Brahman*, and as *Shariraka Sutras* because they deal with the nature of the unconditioned *Atman* embodied in human form.

20. The distinction between *Ishwara* and *Brahman* is quite akin to Paul Tillich's distinction between *God* and *God-beyond-God*, and Eckhart's *Deus* and *Deitas*.

21. A. K. Coomaraswamy, *Hinduism and Buddhism* (New York: Philosophical Library, n.d.), p. 54n.

22. *Dhammapada* 160.

23. *Samyutta-Nikaya* III.143.

24. See A. K. Coomaraswamy, *op. cit.* for a succinct defense of the thesis that the Buddhist tradition is essentially a continuation of the Brahmanic tradition.

25. Swami Sardananda, *op. cit,* pp. 319-20.

26. Swami Vivekananda, *The Complete Works of Swami Vivekananda*, Vol. IV (Mayavati: Advaita Ashram, 1932), pp. 182-3.
27. *Anguttara-Nikaya* IV.
28. *Maha-parinibbana Sutta* II.33.

CHAPTER 4

1. Psalms 121.
2. *Hagiga* 5a and *Sanhedrin* 38b; cited in E. Fromm, *op. cit.*, p. 172. He goes on to mention that "the rabbinic tradition is well aware of the difference in the use of YHWH (The Lord) and Elohim (God). While modern critics of the Scriptures have used this difference as the key to discover the basic literary sources of the Bible, the rabbinic view has made this interpretation: YHWH denotes God under His attribute of compassion; Elohim under the attribute of justice."
3. Genesis 17:1-2; 15:1.
4. Martin Buber, *The Prophetic Faith* (New York: Harper and Row, 1960), pp. 35-36.
5. *Ibid.*, p. 36.
6. Greek *prophetes*, to speak for, to be an instrument of.
7. Jeremiah 1:9.
8. Exodus 3:9-20.
9. Genesis 32:28.
10. For example in Exodus 32:27 and Matthew 15:31.
11. Matthew 15:24.
12. Huston Smith, *The Religions of Man* (New York: Harper and Row, 1958), p. 339.
13. See Rudolf Bultmann, *Primitive Christianity* (London: Collins, 1956), p. 223.
14. For example, Martin Buber, *Two Types of Faith* (New York: Harper Torchbook, 1961), see especially pp. 7-12.
15. Exodus 3:14.
16. Romans 14:23.
17. With reference to Christianity, see Bultmann, *op. cit.*, p. 239.
18. Genesis 3:22-24.
19. At least this is so with Paul; see Bultmann, *op. cit.*, footnote on p. 239.
20. Ecclesiastes 12:13-14.
21. Genesis 3:1-9.
22. Isaiah 40:6-8.
23. Quoted by C. G. Jung, *op. cit*, p. 482. Similar sentiments are expressed in Job (9:1) and Romans (3:20).

24. However, see E. Fromm, *op. cit.*, for a radically different interpretation of the Old Testament.
25. I Thessalonians 5:17.
26. John 10:30-33.
27. See R. C. Zaehner, *The Comparison of Religions* (Boston: Beacon Press, 1962), p. 171.
28. Soren Kierkegaard, "Man's Need of God Constitutes his Highest Perfection" in his *Edifying Discourses* (New York: Fontana Books, 1958), p. 151.
29. Hebrews 11:1.
30. Psalms 46:1.
31. Psalms 62:1, 5-6.
32. I Corinthians 13:13.
33. See Rudolf Bultmann, *op cit.*, p. 94.
34. Mark 1:15.
35. Matthew 19:27-29.
36. Matthew 23:33.
37. I Corinthians 13:13.
38. James 2:14, 19-20.
39. Matthew 25:34-40. *The Holy Bible*, Revised Standard Version, *op. cit.*
40. I Corinthians 13:3, 8.
41. John 3:16.
42. This particular translation of Philippians 2:6-8 is J. B. Phillips, *The New Testament in Modern English* (London: Geoffrey Bles, 1960), pp. 412-13.
43. John 15:13.
44. Deuteronomy 6:5.
45. Deuteronomy 7:8.
46. Deuteronomy 10:12.
47. Deuteronomy 10:12, 13, 20; 11:1, 22:13:5, 14; 19:9.
48. Leviticus 19:2; Matthew 5:48; Luke 6:36.
49. Matthew 22:36-40.
50. Galatians 5:14.
51. Romans 7:5; Acts 3:10.
52. Matthew 18:3.
53. Colossians 2:19.
54. II Corinthians 5:6; Luke 13:3.
55. Matthew 6:28-33. *The Holy Bible*, Revised Standard Version, *op cit.*

CHAPTER 5

1. Psalms 119:19; John 17:14-16.

2. Alexei Tolstoy, *Memoires of a Mad Man*, trans. by A. Maude (New York: World Classics, n.d.).

3. Quoted by S. Radhakrishnan, "The Indian Approach to the Religious Problem" in C. A. Moore, ed., *The Indian Mind* (Honolulu: East-West Centre Press, 1967), p. 75.

4. I John 5:19.

5. For a short discussion of parallelism between existentialist and Indian thought, see K. Guru Dutt, *Existentialism and Indian Thought* (New York: Wisdom Library, 1960), p. 50. For a discussion of the thoughts of Gabriel Marcel and the Buddha, see Sally Donnelly, "Marcel and Buddha: A Metaphysics of Enlightenment," *The Journal of Religious Thought* XXIV (1967-68), pp. 51-81.

6. Romans 7:24.

7. *Brihadaranyak Upanishad* I.3.28.

8. Quoted in Colin Wilson, *The Outsider* (London: Pan Books, 1963), p. 25.

9. Quoted in Nancy Wilson Ross, ed., *The World of Zen* (New York: Random House, 1960), p. 239.

10. See Romans 5:12-14 and Psalms 51:5 for examples.

11. I Peter 2:11, I Chronicles 29:15; Hebrews 13:14; 11:10.

12. Rabindranath Tagore, *Gitanjali* (with an introduction by W. B. Yeats) (Boston: International Pocket Library, n.d.), poem 30.

13. Romans 14:23.

14. Mark 14:36.

15. Luke 18:10-14.

16. Quoted in S. Radhakrishnan, *The Principal Upanishads* (New York: Harper & Brothers, 1953), p. 128, footnote 3.

17. Quoted in N. W. Ross, *op. cit.*, p. 248.

18. Sri Aurobindo, "The Guest," in his *Last Poems* (Pondicherry: Sri Aurobindo Ashram, 1952).

19. *Shiva Gita* 13:32.

20. *One Hundred Poems of Kabir*, *op. cit.*, poem III.

21. *Mandukya Upanishad* 7.

22. *Mundaka Upanishad* I.i:4-5.

23. *Dhammapada* XX.282.

24. P. T. Raju, "The Concept of Man in Indian Thought," in S. Radhakrishnan and P. T. Raju, eds., *The Concept of Man* (London: George Allen & Unwin, 1966), p. 302.

25. For example, on p. 114 of Shankara's *Viveka-Chudamani (Crest-Jewel of Discrimination)*, trans. by Swami Prabhavananda and C. Isherwood (Hollywood: Vedanta Press, 1947). This particular expression is used numerous times in this work and in the *Brihadaranyaka Upanishad* (I.4:10), and elsewhere.

26. The four *great utterances* are: "Thou art that," *tat tvam asi* *(Chandogya Upanishad* 6:9ff.); "This *Atman* is *Brahman*," *ayam itma brahman (Mandukya Up.* 2); "I am *Brahman*" *aham brahmasmi (Brihadaranyaka Up.* I.4:10); and "Consciousness is *Brahman*" *Prajnanam brahman (Aitareya Up.* 5:3).

27. *Mundaka Upanishad* 3.2:9.

28. *Enneads* VI 9 (9), Ch. 9f.

29. Hendrik Kraemer, *Religion and the Christian Faith* (London: 1956), p. 335; cited in R. C. Zaehner, *op. cit.,* p. 14.

30. Quoted in Aldous Huxley, *op. cit.,* 25.

31. Rudolph Otto, *Mysticism East and West* (New York: Collier Books, 1962), p. 199.

32. John 17:21.

33. See Walter Nigg, *The Heretics* (New York: Alfred A. Knopf, 1962) for a brief account of some well-known heretics; many of these were mystics, including the ones mentioned here.

34. See R. C. Zaehner, *Mysticism—Sacred and Profane* (New York, London: Oxford Univ. Press, 1961), especially pp. 198-207 where he tries to maintain the superiority of the monotheistic mysticism over the monistic. In India different schools regard one or the other as superior.

35. In this connection, see Ninian Smart, "Interpretation and Mystical Experience," *Religious Studies,* I (1966), pp. 75-87.

36. For example, D. Lamont, *Christ and the World of Thought,* p. 180, cited in Sidney Spencer, *Mysticism in World Religion* (Penguin Books, 1963), p. 340.

37. For an interesting comparison, although excessively psychologistic, see Isidor Thorner, "Prophetic and Mystic Experience: Comparison and Consequences," *Jour. Scientific Study of Religion,* V (1965), p. 82-96.

38. *Bhagavad Gita* 4:7-8.

39. See H. Zimmer, *Myths and Symbols in Indian Art and Civilization,* Ed. by J. Campbell. (New York: Harper Torchbooks, 1962), pp. 82-88.

40. *Brahmavaivarta Purana;* quoted in Zimmer, *op. cit.,* chapter 1.

41. For some discussion of the contrasting views about *time* and *history* in the two traditions, see R. Ravindra, "Time in Christian and Indian Traditions," *Dalhousie Review,* 51, (1971), pp. 5-17.

42. For a detailed discussion of the Judaeo-Christian philosophies of history, see S. G. F. Brandon, *History, Time and Deity* (New York: Barnes and Noble, 1965), chapters 5 and 6.

43. *In Memoriam,* Conclusion, stanza 36.

126 Notes to Chapter 5

44. See Oscar Cullman, *Christ and Time*, trans. by F. V. Wilson (London: SCM Press, 1951), pp. 51-60.
45. Quoted by Lynn White, Jr., "Christian Myth and Christian History," *Jour. of History of Ideas*, 3 (1942), pp. 147-158.
46. Brandon, *op. cit.*, pp. 204-5.
47. John 3:16; Philippians 2:6.
48. *Commentary on the Brahma Sutra* (iv. 1.3).
49. "India's propensity for transcendental pursuit and the misery of India's history are, most certainly, intimately related to each other; they must not be regarded separately."—H. Zimmer, *Philosophies of India* (New York: World Publ., 1956), p. 83. In this connection, also see S. Radhakrishnan, *Eastern Religion and Western Thought* (New York: Galaxy Books, 1959), pp. 257-259.
50. Quoted in Radhakrishnan and Raju, eds., *op cit.*, p. 23.
51. Ephesians 2:8-9.
52. Philippians 2:12-13.
53. Psalms 23:1-6.
54. See the first chapter for the parable told by Ramakrishna, illustrating precisely this point.
55. Matthew 16:15-19.
56. *Mahaparinibbana Sutta* II.33.

CHAPTER 6

1. I. Thessalonians, 5:24.
2. Jacob Boehme, *A Dialogue between a Scholar and his Master concerning the Supersensual Life*, Dialogue I.
3. Luke, 17:21.
4. *Mundaka Upanishad* 2.1:10.
5. *Moralia*, 384 D.f.
6. *Shvetashvatara Upanishad* 2:15.
7. *Enneads* V.3.9.
8. Quoted in F. C. Happold, *Mysticism* (Penguin, 1967), pp. 174-75.
9. Isaiah, 57:20.
10. Pascal's *Pensees* with an English translation, brief notes and introduction by H. F. Stewart (New York: The Modern Library, n.d.), p. 91.
11. J. Ancelet-Eustache, *Master Eckhart and the Rheineland Mystics*, trans. by H. Graef (New York: Harper Torchbook, n.d.), p. 66; second part quoted in Aldous Huxley, *The Perennial Philosophy* (New York: Fontana Books, 1958), p. 24.
12. *Chandogya Upanishad*, 6:9ff and *Mandukya Upanishad*, 2.
13. John 10:30: 14:6.
14. *Enneads* VI.9.11.

15. Matthew 11:28.
16. *Bhagavad Gita* 18:66.
17. *Samyutta Nikaya* 2:106.
18. *Brihadaranyaka Upanishad* 44:8.
19. Hebrews 5:1-10.
20. This is the reason why sacred works of art often do not carry author's names. Fra Angelico said: "Not I have painted but He painted through me." Similarly, Dante, the author of the *Divine Comedy*, and Vyas, the author of the *Mahabharata*, considered themselves only writing down what was being dictated from above.
21. John 12:49.
22. *Majjhima Nikaya* 1:68f.
23. This is one of the more than five hundred sayings of Kabir included in the *Gurugranth Sahib*, the holy book of the Sikhs.
24. I Corinthians 3:18-20.
25. Sri Aurobindo's, "Liberation," in *Last Poems, op. cit.*
26. This imbalance of sensibilities is endemic in academic life. The classic expression of this is the well-known phrase of Descartes, the father of modern philosophy, viz., *cogito ergo sum* (I think therefore I am), as if thinking were a disembodied activity without any relation to sensation, feeling, and purpose.
27. *The Republic* 443.
28. *Brihadaranyaka Upanishad* 3.6:1.
29. *Majjhima Nikaya* 63.
30. This attitude of pursuing "science," "art," or "philosophy" for its own sake is a characteristic of the modern mind and is often explicitly admitted and prized. However, it is quite opposed to the sacred point of view according to which all of these activities have significance only to the extent that they bring their practitioners closer to the Divine.
31. *Majjhima Nikaya*, 1. It is instructive to recall that Isaac Newton in his *Principia* also made a similar comment: *hypotheses non fingo* (I feign no hypotheses). Obviously, he could not have been against scientific theorizing, for precisely that is what he was doing in the book. It was empty, metaphysical speculation that he was against because he regarded it as unfruitful and not likely to lead to progress in Physics; only those assertions were worth scientific consideration which directly or indirectly were subject to an experimental check. Similarly, in the sacred science of spiritual becoming, only those assertions are worthy of consideration which are subject to experiential verification.
32. Quoted in Rudolph Otto, *Mysticism East and West, op. cit.*, p. 43.
33. Quoted by Nietzsche in *The Gay Science*, aphorism 292.

34. *Majjhima Nikaya* 72.

35. S. Radhakrishnan, trans. and ed., *The Principal Upanishads*. (New York: Harper & Brothers, 1953), p. 145n.

36. *Lankavatara Sutra*.

37. *The Poems of St. John of the Cross*; trans. by Willis Barnstone, (New York: New Directions, 1972). The poem entitled "I came into the unknown."

38. One of the best known works in modern philosophy of science is Karl Popper's *Conjectures and Refutations*, where this point of view is maintained.

39. See Thomas Kuhn, *The Structure of Scientific Revolution* (University of Chicago Press, 1962) for a discussion of this point.

40. Immanuel Kant, *Critique of Pure Reason*, trans. by F. Max Muller, preface to the second edition. A similar appreciation of the scientific method is evident in the writings of Francis Bacon, the patron saint of the Royal Society. He writes, for example, "Nature should not only be studied 'free and at large (when she is left to her own course...)' but should be studied even more when 'under constraint,' when 'by art and the hand of man, she is forced out of her natural state and squeezed and moulded.'" (*Instauratio Magna* in *The Works Of Francis Bacon*, ed. by J. Spedding, R. L. Ellis, and D. Herth. London, 1857-74, 14 volumes), Vol. V, p. 145.

41. Many students of nature have misunderstood this point. For example, Thomas Huxley says: "Science seems to me to teach in the highest and strongest manners the great truth which is embodied in the Christian conception of entire surrender to the will of God. Sit down before a fact as a little child, be prepared to give up every preconceived notion, follow humbly wherever and to whatever abyss Nature leads, or you shall learn nothing." (L. Huxley, *Life and Letters of Thomas Henry Huxley*, 3 vols. London, 1963, Vol. I, p. 316.) Similarly, M. Unamuno: "Science teaches us, in effect, to submit our reason to the truth and to know and judge of things as they are—that is to say, as they themselves choose to be and not as we would have them be." (*The Tragic Sense of Life* trans. by Flitch. London: Macmillan, 1931), p. 197.

42. In this connection, see the following papers by the author: "Experience and Experiment: A Critique of Modern Scientific Knowing," *Dalhousie Review*, Vol. 55, 1975-76, pp. 655-674; "Western Science and Technology and the Indian Intellectual Tradition," *Manthan*, Sept. 1978; and "Perception in Yoga and Physics," *Re-Vision*, Vol. 3, 1980, pp. 36-42.

43. Ruth Moore, *Neils Bohr* (New York: Alfred A. Knopf, 1966), p. 406.

44. As long as this non-sacred point of view does not take hold of men, science in the modern sense cannot arise; in any case, it

cannot become the dominant value which it is for the modern world. It is to be expected that science could not develop much in China, India, or medieval Christendom. The sweeping profanization of Europe in the 15th-17th centuries—of which the Renaissance humanism is an instance—was a necessary prerequisite for the rise of modern science based on control and manipulation.

45. *Chandogya Upanishad* VII 6:1.

46. Matthew 11:27.

47. S. Radhakrishnan, *The Principal Upanishads. Op. cit.*, p. 99n.

48. *Gandharva Tantra.*

49. John 3:13.

50. The difficulty in understanding Einstein's Theory of General Relativity is proverbial in physics circles. It used to be said in the early twenties that only three persons really understood this theory. Somebody mentioned this to Arthur Eddington, the great English mathematical physicist who was among the first supporters of Einstein. Eddington thought for a long time, then said, "I wonder who the third one is."

51. *Katha Upanishad* 1.2:24.

52. Ecclesiasticus 19:4.

53. This list is originally due to Gregory the Great (540-604 A.D.). The list has varied somewhat through the centuries but has remained substantially the same.

54. *Bhagavad Gita* 16:21.

55. *Buddhist Legends*, translated from the original Pali text of the *Dhammapada* commentary by E. W. Burlingame (The Pali Text Society, 1969), Part 1, pp. 11-12. (This is Vol. 28 in the Harvard Oriental Series).

56. Scholars have long argued about the possible connections between many striking parallels occurring in Buddhist and Christian legends. It is likely that St Luke was familiar with Buddhist scriptures. For details and references, see ibid., pp. 9-14.

57. Compare: "Many are called but few are chosen," (Matthew 22:14).

58. Matthew 7:13-14.

59. Matthew 26:39.

60. *Bhagavad Gita* 16:1-4.

61. *Brihadaranyaka Upanishad* 4.3:22.

62. Quoted in A. K. Coomaraswamy, "The Pilgrim's Way," *Jour. Bihar & Orissa Research Society*, V. 23, 1927, pp. 452-71.

63. J. Krishnamurti, *Commentaries on Living 3rd Series*, edited by D. Rajagopal (Wheaton: Theosophical Publishing House, 1960), p. 82.

64. Plotinus, *Enneads* I. 6.9. Compare Goethe:
    Waer' nicht das Auge sonnenhaft,
    Die Sonne koennt' es nie erblicken.
    Laeg' nicht in uns des Gottes eigene Kraft,
    Wie koennt' uns Goettliches entzuecken?

    (If the eye were not sensitive to the sun,
    It could not perceive that sun.
    If God's own power did not lie within us,
    How could the divine enchant us?)

65. Matthew 13:12; Plotinus, *Enneads* V. 3.8.
66. In this connection, see Hans Jacob, *Modern Psychotherapy and Hindu Sadhana* (London: Allen and Unwin, 1961); René Guénon, *The Reign of Quantity*; R. E. A. Johansson, *The Psychology of Nirvana* (London: Allen and Unwin, 1969); and R. Ravindra, "Is Religion Psychotherapy? An Indian View," *Religious Studies*, V. 14, 1978.
67. Ephesians 6:12.
68. Matthew 12:30.
69. *Maitri Upanishad* 6.34:3.
70. Colossians 1:20.
71. I John 5:18.
72. G. I. Gurdjieff, *All and Everything: Beelzebub's Tales to His Grandson* (New York: E. P. Dutton, 1964), p. 418. Practitioners of primary activities—science, art and spirituality—have always been suspicious of those who talk about these activities without producing the corresponding works in science, art, or spirit. Einstein once wrote to Peter Kapitsa, "When I study philosophical works, I feel I am swallowing something which I don't have in my mouth."
73. I Corinthians 4:20.
74. Psalms 1:4.
75. Romans 7:15-20.
76. *Bhagavad Gita* 3:36.

Glossary of Indian Words

Ahamkara: Egotism, self-consciousness, pride; literally, "I am the doer."

Asur: antigod, demon, an evil spirit

Atman: Self, Spirit, soul, the deepest part of a person

Avatar: descent of a deity; incarnation (particularly of Vishnu, the maintainer of cosmic order)

Avidya: ignorance, illusion (personified as *Maya*)

Bhagavad Gita: Song of the Blessed One; perhaps the single most important work to originate from India—part of the great epic *Mahabharata*; dated approximately 600-200 B.C.

Bhakti: devotion, adoration, worship, love

Bodhi: perfect knowledge or wisdom (by which a man becomes Buddha)

Brahma: first of the triad of personal Gods Brahma-Vishnu-Shiva; Universal Spirit manifested as a personal Creator; the Great Being

Brahman: Godhead, *Deitas*, Absolute, self-existent non-personal Spirit; the Ultimate Reality; Vastness

Brahmin: one who has sacred knowledge; a man belonging to the first of the four castes

Buddha: awakened, awake, enlightened, liberated; used as a proper name of the historical Siddhartha Gautama

Buddhi: soul, will, intellect, integrated intelligence, understanding; see footnote 17, Chapter 1 for details

Darshana: point of view; perspective, school of philosophy

Dhammapada: an early Buddhist document discussing the chief values of life and the path which leads to enlightenment

Dharma: law, order, responsibility for the maintenance of order, duty, religion, righteousness, obligation

Dukkha: suffering, anguish, *angst*, affliction, sorrow

Guna: strand, constituent; three gunas—*sattva, rajas, tamas*—are the three fundamental constituents of the whole prakriti (nature) even at the subtlest level.

Ishwara: God, the supreme Being, personal Deity

Jnana: wisdom, sacred knowledge (as opposed to *vijnana* which is profane knowledge, science)

Kala: time; also identified with *Yama* (death); the root word is *kal* which means to calculate or enumerate

Kama: wish, desire, longing; sexual love or desire personified

Karma: act, action, work; result, effect; law of *karma* (cause and effect) is cosmic, i.e., applied to moral psychological as well as physical spheres

Manas: mind, reason; faculty by which objects of sense affect *buddhi*

Maya: illusion, unreality, deception; illusion personified, identified with *prakriti*; power; from the same root as measuring

Moksha: emancipation, liberation, deliverance

Mukti: freedom, liberation, final beatitude; same as *moksha*

Nirvana: perfect calm or repose, extinction (*of dukkha*), cessation (of *trishna*)

Prakriti: Nature; materiality; same as Maya

Purusha: person, primeval man, Supreme Being, also identified with Atman and Brahman

Sadhana: accomplishing, realization, practice, fulfillment, completion

Samadhi: putting together, joining, synthesis, composure; integration; profound meditation; the eighth and last state of yoga

Samsara: world, secular life, worldly illusion; circuit of mundane existence; the cosmic flux

Shiva: auspicious; lord of sleep; third of the Hindu triad of personal gods, Brahma-Vishnu-Shiva; lord of destruction and reassimilation, and of transformation

Tapas: heat; religious austerity, penance, effort

Tathagata: another name of the Buddha; literally, thus gone

Trishna: longing, egoistic craving, desire

Turiya: the fourth (state of consciousness) as distinguished from dreamless sleep, dreaming, and waking

Upanishad: the sacred writings, usually philosophical in nature, of the Hindus. These constitute the concluding positions of the *Vedas,* and number over 200 different works, dating between 800 and 500 B.C. Among the most important *Upanishads* are: *Isha, Kena, Katha, Mundaka, Prashna, Mandukya, Taittiriya, Aitareya, Chandogya, Brihadaranyaka, Shvetashvatara,* and the *Maitri.*

Veda: the most sacred literature of the Hindus; knowledge. There are four *Vedas,* the oldest being the *Rig Veda,* composed around 1200 B.C.

Vedanta: end of knowledge; end of the Veda; most influential school of philosophy in India

Vishnu: second of the Hindu triad of gods, Brahma-Vishnu-Shiva; the preserver and the sustainer

Yajna: worship; a sacrificial rite or ceremony

Yoga: the art of yoking, joining, attaching; meditation with the aim of union with *Ishwara* or the Supreme Spirit; generally any path for such union

Selected Bibliography

Aurobindo, Sri. *Collected Poems.* Pondicherry: Sri Aurobindo Ashram, 1979.

————. *The Upanishads.* Pondicherry: Sri Aurobindo Ashram, 1981.

Buber, Martin. *Ten Rungs: Hasidic Sayings.* New York: Schocken Press, 1962.

Chatterji, J. C. *Wisdom of the Vedas.* Wheaton: Theosophical Publishing House, 1980.

Conze, Edward, trans. *Buddhist Scriptures.* Penguin Classic, 1959.

Coomaraswamy, A. K. *Hinduism and Buddhism.* Brooklyn: Greenwood House, 1971.

Daumal, René. *Mt. Analogue,* trans. Roger Shattuck. New York: Penguin Books, 1974.

The Dhammapada, trans. I. Babbit. New York: New Directions, 1965.

Eliot, T. S. *Four Quartets.*

Fromm, Erich. *You Shall Be as Gods.* New York: Fawcett, 1977.

Humphreys, Christmas. *Exploring Buddhism.* Wheaton, IL: Theosophical Publishing House, 1975.

Huxley, Aldous. *The Perennial Philosophy.* New York: Harper and Row, 1970.

Kabir. *Forty-four of the Ecstatic Poems of Kabir,* trans. Robert Bly. Boston: Beacon Press, 1977.

Krishnamurti, J. *Commentaries on Living, 3rd Series,* ed. D. Rajagopal. Wheaton, IL: Theosophical Publishing House, 1967.

Needleman, Jacob. *The Heart of Philosophy.* New York: Bantam Books, 1982.

136   *Selected Bibliography*

——. *Lost Christianity*. New York: Doubleday, 1980.

The New English Bible with the Apocrypha. Oxford University Press and Cambridge University Press, 1970.

Nikhilananda, Swami. *The Gospel of Shri Ramakrishna*. Madras: Mylapore, 1947.

Ouspensky, P. D. *In Search of the Miraculous—Fragments of an Unknown Teaching*. New York: Harcourt Brace Jovanavich, 1965.

Patanjali. *How to Know God: The Yoga Aphorisms of Patanjali*, trans. Swami Prabhavananda and C. Isherwood. New York: New American Library, 1969.

Prabhavananda, Swami. *The Spiritual Heritage of India*. Hollywood: Vedanta Press, 1979.

Radhakrishnan, S., trans. and ed. *The Principal Upanishads*. Atlantic Highlands, NJ: Humanities Press, 1978.

Ross, Nancy Wilson, ed. *The World of Zen*. New York: Random House, 1960.

Smith, Huston. *Forgotten Truth*. New York: Harper & Row, 1977.

——. The Religions of Man. New York: Harper and Row, 1965.

Suzuki, D. T. *Essays in Zen Buddhism*. New York: Grove Press, 1961.

Tagore, Rabindranath. *Gitanjali*. New York: Macmillan, 1971.

Von Durckheim, Karlfried Graf. The Way of Transformation: Daily Life as Spiritual Exercise. London: Mandala Books, Unwin Paperbacks, 1980.

Williams, Jay G. *Yeshua Buddha*. Wheaton, IL: Theosophical Publishing House, 1978.

Zaehner, R. C. *Mysticism—Sacred and Profane*. New York: Oxford University Press, 1961.

——, ed. *The Bhagavad-Gita*. New York: Oxford University Press, 1969.

Zimmer, Heinrich. *Myths and Symbols in Indian Art and Civilization*, ed. Joseph Campbell. Bollingen Series, Vol. 6. Princeton: Princeton Univ. Press, 1971.

Index

Anxiety, 6, 8
Atman, 2, 5, 11, 40, 41, 64, 77,
    131; and Brahman, 29, 31,
    35-38, 62, 65, 86, 104, 112
Avatara, 70-72
Awakening, 3-6, 19, 23, 39,
    112, 115

Biblical tradition. See Judaeo-
    Christian tradition
Brahman, 17, 27, 63-66, 67, 78,
    81, 85, 87, 120; and Atman,
    29, 31, 35-38, 62, 86, 112;
    and maya, 111
Buddha, 14, 22, 39-40, 42, 62,
    79, 82, 87, 88, 92, 124;
    tempted, 105
Buddhi, 11, 12, 118-119

Charity, 52, 53
Christ, 6, 7, 26, 50, 69, 70, 73,
    74, 82, 88, 103, 110, 112
Consciousness, 16, 87, 96, 98,
    103, 109; fourth state of, 63;
    levels of, 64, 85; ordinary,
    15; states of, 28, 111; and
    transcendental experience,
    41
Covenant, 44, 47, 72

Damnation, 52, 69, 76
Death, 57, 58, 71, 72

Deliverance, 63, 66, 77, 93.
    See also Freedom,
    Liberation
Dharma, 40, 70, 71
Dualism, 76, 77
Dualities, 111
Dukkha, 4, 7, 40, 59

Eastern tradition. See Hindu-
    Buddhist tradition
Effort, 3, 32, 33, 34, 42, 89, 109,
    111; and grace, 49, 50;
    individual's 25; without
    violence, 102
Ego, 6-12, 60, 61, 77, 89, 95,
    107; surrender of 6, 12-18,
    87, 109, 115. See also Self-
    will and Self-surrender
Enlightenment, 39, 60, 75, 81.
    See also Liberation
Eternal, 88
Eternity, 13-17, 73, 76

Faith, 47-48, 50, 51, 52, 55, 56,
    61, 75, 79, 81; and doubt, 52
Freedom, 42, 57, 59, 62, 63, 77,
    81. See also Liberation

God's Community, 46-47
Grace, 3, 31, 32, 48, 50, 51, 55,
    75, 79, 81
Great Utterance, 66, 125

137

Hindu-Buddhist tradition, xi,
27, 28-42; and Judaeo-
Christian tradition, x-xiii, 27,
57-82
Hope, 51, 52, 58, 75; and
fears, 52
Human, condition, 3, 58, 59,
82, 109, 114; Liberation, 4,
18, 39, 81, 93, 114; -nature
(dual), 9, 12-14

I AM, 2, 46, 48, 117
I am, 11, 117
Identity, 4-5, 14-15, 104
Indian tradition. *See* Hindu-
Buddhist tradition
Individualism, 10, 76

Judaeo-Christian tradition, xi,
27, 43-56; and Hindu-
Buddhist tradition, x-xiii, 27,
57-82

Karma, 10, 27, 64, 78
Knowledge, as transformation,
xi, 15, 36, 65, 66, 75; higher
and lower, 63, 95-99;
objective, 97-101

Liberation, xii, 6, 15, 17, 36,
38, 40-42, 65, 75, 81, 93, 106.
See also Deliverance,
Freedom, Moksha, Nirvana
Living God, ix, 45, 61, 82
Love, 17, 51, 53-65, 64

Maya, 4, 15, 75, 77, 111, 113
Meditation, 33, 63, 64, 75, 81,
101-102
Moksha, 28, 75, 132. *See also*
Liberation, Nirvana
Mysticism, 50, 66-69, 75, 100;
Monistic, 66, 67, 68;
Monotheistic, 68
Mystery, xiv, 94, 97

Nirvana, 22, 28, 36, 40, 81,
111, 112, 113. *See also*
Liberation, Moksha

Opposites, reconciling, 109-
112

Person, 1, 10, 18, 45, 62, 65
Personality, 1, 2, 62, 80
Philosophy and Spirit, xiii, 36,
90-97
Prayer, 75, 81
Preparation, 103-106
Prophet, 12, 21, 44, 45, 51, 69,
75, 76, 79
Prophetism, 69-70, 75
Psychic powers, 110
Psychology and Spirit, xiii, 109
Psychotherapy and spiritual
paths, 109

Reason and Spirit, 90-95,
99-101
Rebirth and Liberation, xii, 5,
13, 21
Redemption, 49, 50, 51, 55, 65.
See also Salvation
Religion, as a veil, xi, 20-27;
levels of, x; and Spiritual
Quest, xiii, 19-26, 42
Reorientation, xii, 5, 13, 23, 55,
107, 109, 113
Repentance, 55, 81. *See also*
Reorientation
Revelation, 44, 46, 66, 69, 75,
76, 77, 79

Sacrifice, 31, 33-34, 78, 89, 96
Salvation, 49, 51, 55, 59, 60, 68,
69, 74-78, 79, 81; and faith,
50; from sin to, 57. *See also*
Redemption
Samadhi, 28, 64, 65, 75
Science and Spirit, xiii, 2,
97-101

Second birth, 6, 8, 14, 21, 61, 89, 96, 112
Self, 2, 6, 29, 40, 61, 63, 81, 86, 87, 93, 103, 111; as initiator, 9; as instrument, 9, 12; lower and higher, 5, 8, 12-14, 40
Self-discovery, 40
Self-forgetting, 4-5
Self-knowledge, ix, 1-6, 25, 81, 84-88
Self-realization, 10, 14, 36, 78, 81, 84, 102
Self-remembering, 5
Self-surrender (or surrender of ego-self), xii, 6, 12-18, 37, 61-62, 79, 91, 111
Self-will, 7, 62, 114. *See also* Ego
Sin, 4, 48, 53, 57, 59, 61, 75, 105; greatest, 65; Original, 61, 81; redemption from, 50; and repentance, 55; root-, 66
Sleep, 2, 3, 4, 43, 58, 95, 108
Son of God, 2, 5, 15, 18, 53, 74, 88

Spiritual discipline, path of, xi, 21, 22, 37, 64, 93, 109, 112, 113
Spiritual Search or Quest, ix, 1-18; and religion, 19-26

Third eye, 108
Time, 13-17, 32, 57, 58, 71-74, 76, 78, 88, 121
Transcent God, 49, 74, 81
Transformation, xi, 5, 7, 22, 93, 103, 106-109, 115

Unbridgeable gap between God and man, 48-50, 66-69, 74, 81

Vedanta, 38, 65, 66, 67

Western tradition. *See* Judaeo-Christian tradition
Who am I: ix, x, xiv, 1-6, 35, 40

Yoga, 25, 31, 37, 38, 64, 75, 109

Zen, 8, 60, 109